Directed

Steps of Peace
in Times of Transition

ALSO BY BRENDA PACE

Journey of a Military Wife
    Dedicated: Steps of Faith in God's Plan
    Devoted: Steps of Love Toward Healthy Relationships
    Deployed: Steps of Hope in Times of Uncertainty
    Directed: Steps of Peace in Times of Transition

Medals Above My Heart: The Rewards of Being a Military Wife
(Coauthored with Carol McGlothlin)

The One Year Yellow Ribbon Devotional: Take a Stand
in Prayer for Our Nation and Those Who Serve
(Coauthored with Carol McGlothlin)

Directed

Steps of Peace
in Times of Transition

BRENDA PACE

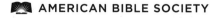 AMERICAN BIBLE SOCIETY

Philadelphia

DIRECTED: STEPS OF PEACE IN TIMES OF TRANSITION
(JOURNEY OF A MILITARY WIFE SERIES)

By Brenda Pace
Edited by Peter Edman, Davina Mc Donald, Art Pace, and Stacey Wright

© 2016 American Bible Society

ISBN 978-1-941448-60-1
ABS Item 124541

Design by Jordan Grove
Cover image by Joshua Wann

Set in Arno Pro and Avenir

American Bible Society
101 North Independence Mall East
Philadelphia, PA 19106

www.american.bible

Printed in the United States of America

Contents

An online version of JOURNEY OF A MILITARY WIFE is also available. You can find this book series, small group study guides, and a place to invite others to share this journey with you at www.MilitaryWife.bible.

Journey 1

Determined to Thrive in Relocation

Introduction

Relocation and its corresponding issues are among the top stresses of life,[1] so military families have regular dates with stress! Issues associated with frequent moves are among the most popular topics in military family forums. A military PCS (Permanent Change of Station) is the classroom of learning to be content. The choice to fight against the circumstances that accompany relocation is ours. Too often, I have allowed complaint and comparison to rob me of the joy and peace of the moment. I forget that I choose the lens through which I view my circumstances.

During this thirty-day journey, we will study biblical examples of people God moved from place to place. God's presence during times of relocation can bring peace in the midst of change. The Bible assures us that God will direct our paths (Proverbs 3:5–6). Every military wife will have a PCS story to share—good or bad. Uncle Sam may order where and when those stories will take place, but he does not control our peace. That part of the story is ours to determine with the help of the Lord.

Each day, you will find a devotional waypoint. A *waypoint* is a stopping place on a journey. Waypoints may be places where you want to return, or they may be significant landmarks. The waypoints you encounter on this journey will help you focus prayerfully on a theme or questionthat can enhance your dedication to God and your understanding of God's purpose for you. Start each day with this prayer: Lord, "Open my eyes, that I may behold wondrous things out of your law" (Psalm 119:18).

Why not join with some fellow sojourners to study God's Word together? As a companion to this book you will find at www.MilitaryWife.bible a set of Bible studies complete with leader and participant notes to guide your discussion.

Welcome to the journey! Let's get moving!

Waypoint 1
A change of course

And Jesse made seven of his sons pass before Samuel. And Samuel said to Jesse, "The LORD has not chosen these." Then Samuel said to Jesse, "Are all your sons here?" And he said, "There remains yet the youngest, but behold, he is keeping the sheep." And Samuel said to Jesse, "Send and get him, for we will not sit down till he comes here." And he sent out and brought him in. Now he was ruddy and had beautiful eyes and was handsome. And the LORD said, "Arise, anoint him, for this is he." Then Samuel took the horn of oil and anointed him in the midst of his brothers. And the Spirit of the LORD rushed upon David from that day forward. And Samuel rose up and went to Ramah. (1 Samuel 16:10–13)

Reflect

The day the prophet Samuel knocked on the door of Jesse's home changed David's life forever. God had sent Samuel to recruit the one he had chosen to be Israel's next king. Instead of a signature on an official form, Samuel sealed the deal by pouring oil on David's head. The anointing of oil carried a contractual or covenantal significance between God and David.[2]

As with David, the day your husband signed his name on Uncle Sam's dotted line changed the course of his life—and yours. God used a prophet with David, but the Lord can just as easily use a military recruiter to set you on a new path.

It is probable that with the oil still dripping from his chin, David began to mentally and spiritually pack his bags for the inevitable first move. Recruiters say, "Join the military and see the world." The world is a big place. After your husband raised his right hand, and before the movers knocked on your door, the important question was, "Where are we going first?"

The verbal picture the recruiter painted of your first assignment location likely looked different from what was printed in black and white on the contract above your husband's signature. David probably asked himself some of the same questions you did. After all, Samuel anointed David to be king when he was still too young to enlist in the military, and he did not become king until he was thirty years old.[3] David, and eventually his family, made multiple moves before he unpacked his bags in the palace.

Sister, God authorized each step of David's journey from unnoticed shepherd boy to king. He was at work in all the awkward situations and moves in which David found himself. When Samuel anointed him, David might not have anticipated that packing up and moving, at times with very short notice, would be a necessary aspect of serving as king.

For military families, even though PCS includes the provision of professional packers, the preparation for a PCS move can be awkward and trying. Yes, I heard you shout, "Amen!" This week we will look at a few of David's PCS moves. Perhaps we will learn something that will help us navigate our own PCS process.

Respond
What does 1 Samuel 16:7 tell you about how God views you? What are some of the things PCS season reveals about your concerns and desires?

Prayer for the journey
Lord, guide me today in the way I should go. May my words and actions be pleasing to you as I walk through this day. Give me grace to triumph in any awkward and trying moment. Amen.

Waypoint 2
From pasture to palace

Read

Therefore Saul sent messengers to Jesse and said, "Send me David your son, who is with the sheep." And Jesse took a donkey laden with bread and a skin of wine and a young goat and sent them by David his son to Saul. And David came to Saul and entered his service. And Saul loved him greatly, and he became his armor-bearer. (1 Samuel 16:19–21)

Reflect

David's first PCS was from the pasture to the palace. If David had been married at the time Samuel recruited him to be king, his wife might have pictured in her mind how the furniture would look in a king's palace. However, David's first move in service to his nation was not directly to the office of the Commander-in-Chief. Sometimes the picture in our mind of what a duty station will be like may prove different when the moving truck rolls through the gate. Though David would one day be king, his first headgear was not a crown but that of a servant. He would make several moves before his own family set up house in a palace.

The historic quarters assigned to my family at our first duty station were charming. The charm faded when I met the nocturnal two-inch creatures who thought they were permanent residents. New challenges give us an opportunity to learn new things. My husband found a way to avoid sharing our home with these unwanted occupants—Roach Prufe®!

You cannot know all the details of what to expect when you PCS. The recruiter or military sponsor may have painted a rosy picture of the installation or overestimated how much free time your husband would have to spend with you. Nevertheless, focus on the big picture of God's plan. David's path to the position for which Samuel recruited him had some unexpected turns and detours. Yet, God was mapping out the course for David to follow. One of the keys to David's success was his recognition and reliance on God's plan for his life. He later wrote, "The steps of a man are established by the LORD, when he delights in his way" (Psalm 37:23). Trust him to establish *your* way as well.

Many years later, I still have fond memories of living in that first set of quarters. The other residents (the two-legged kind) were great neighbors, and the community was a perfect place for my two boys to safely play and make friends. God was indeed ordering my family's steps and the place where we laid our heads. As an added bonus, we learned the first thing to do when we signed for quarters—buy some Roach Prufe.

Respond

Read and meditate on Psalm 37:23. In what ways have you seen the Lord establish your way? How are you delighting in the Lord wherever you are in the relocation process?

Prayer for the journey

Lord, thank you for the promise that you will establish the direction of my life. Help me to delight in you today and trust you for my future. Amen.

Waypoint 3
The reward of small talk

Read

As soon as he had finished speaking to Saul, the soul of Jonathan was knit to the soul of David, and Jonathan loved him as his own soul. (1 Samuel 18:1)

Reflect

My birthplace is Tennessee. A southern upbringing instilled the importance of courtesy. (I was actually voted "Most Courteous" in high school.) When I became a military wife, I knew how to be "sweet" and courteous. I could match anyone's small talk and smile no matter what I was thinking. But y'all, I'm a girl who is not content with surface relationships and I wondered how that would jive with the transient nature of military life. Small talk can get tiresome but it is the initial step toward friendship.

I quickly learned that the shared experience of military life is rich soil for friendship to flourish. The idea of moving and going through the process of making friends—*again*—can be exhausting. I felt that way with every PCS move. I often wished I could hand out a "friend résumé" to offset the initial awkward *new girl* stage and skip the small talk. Each time we moved, though, I would polish my "Most Courteous" crown and begin the process of introducing myself—*again*.

Do you know what happened? I found other military wives who wanted to go deeper than small talk. Over the years, I connected with women who shared my joys and frustrations and I made lifelong friends who are like family.

1 Samuel 18:1 notes that Jonathan's soul was *knit* to the soul of David. The use of the word "knit" implies a family-like relationship.[4] The story would make more sense if Jonathan looked at David as a rival, since David had been anointed to be the next king. After all, as King Saul's son, Jonathan was next in line for the throne. Out of jealousy, King Saul wanted to kill David, yet his son made a covenant with David to treat him as a brother. Here, in David's first assignment, he met his best friend for life.

This transient military lifestyle seems the most unlikely place to nurture deep and lasting relationships, but our overlapping lives bind us together. Not everyone will be open to being a friend, but I guarantee someone will be looking for a friend like you! Sister, a new location is a new opportunity for new friendships. If you stay in the military long enough, you may begin to chronicle the places you live by the friends you make in each place. Military installations may close down, but the friends you make will last a lifetime.

Respond

Take some time today and thank God for the lifelong friends you have made in the military. Go one step further and connect with one or more of these friends via text, email, or, better yet, a written note.

Prayer for the journey

Thank you, Lord, for the gift of friendship. Thank you for this military life that has brought me friends who feel like family. Bless my friends today and continue to knit our hearts together. Amen.

Waypoint 4
What 'PCS' really means

David departed from there and escaped to the cave of Adullam. And when his brothers and all his father's house heard it, they went down there to him. And everyone who was in distress, and everyone who was in debt, and everyone who was bitter in soul, gathered to him. And he became commander over them. And there were with him about four hundred men. (1 Samuel 22:1–2)

Reflect

The Department of Defense's acronym for relocation is PCS, which stands for Permanent Change of Station. A PCS normally results in a new job, a new home, a new school, and a new community. You find new places to shop, eat, and explore. Most importantly, you always find new people. Interesting people make up every military community, each with a unique life story to tell. You can research many facts about your next PCS location, but there is one fascinating aspect of your next move that you cannot know until you arrive—the people you will meet. In fact, PCS could stand for *People's Captivating Stories!*

King Saul became jealous of David and his success and sought to kill him. When David fled for his life, he ended up in a wilderness location surrounded by four hundred people who were trying to get away from difficult situations and start a new life. Some of the people were in debt. Others were simply not content with the direction of their lives. A few may have been fleeing from the authorities. The Scriptures paint the notion these folks were passionate for change.[5] Reading about David's associates makes you wonder if they were the first ones to sing the *jody* or cadence call some troops sing today: "Got a letter in the mail; go to war or go to jail." These men joined David and eventually they became known as his "mighty men." They were men who could say, "Don't judge my future from my past."

Recently I rejoiced with a young military wife as she celebrated the completion of a beautiful new home. Building a new home is a major life event, but for this friend, her new home was uncommon. I was privileged to hear her story of growing up, often homeless, with a dim view of the future. In desperation, and as a way out of poverty, she joined the military. She met people in the military who introduced her to Jesus, and today she serves as a faithful leader in her chapel women's ministry. She is one of the many mighty women I am proud to know.

In the military you meet folks from all walks of life that you may never otherwise meet. The military creates community where the paths of people can cross in an environment that produces bonds that tie us together. May I encourage you to share your story and listen to the stories of others? Find those who are eager to create a new future and be *mighty women* of God together.

Respond
Who are some of the people you have met since being a military spouse whom you would not have otherwise encountered? How have these people blessed you?

Prayer for the journey
Lord, thank you for new beginnings. Thank you that in you we can forget what lies behind and strain forward to what lies ahead (Philippians 3:13).

Waypoint 5
Emotional logistics

And David was greatly distressed, for the people spoke of stoning him, because all the people were bitter in soul, each for his sons and daughters. But David strengthened himself in the LORD his God.
(1 Samuel 30:6)

The military offers checklists for the practical logistics of a PCS—before, during, and after. You can download handy lists just begging for red checks regarding everything you need from packing to setting up your new home.[6]

While such lists are helpful, especially for unorganized people like me, I wish there was an Emotional Logistics Checklist. Logistics is a term the military uses for handling the details of an operation. I must admit that a PCS often brings logistics that are hard for me to handle. I need a checklist for getting to the other side of:

- ☐ Grief
- ☐ Isolation
- ☐ Resentment
- ☐ Distress
- ☐ Sadness

No matter what spin you put on the event, one or more of these emotional logistics will accompany your PCS. You cannot deny that moving is a distressing experience.[7]

Relocation can make you feel like an exile with loss of place and person. British military wife Sue Jervis writes of the relocation experience, "There can be few other situations that remove individuals so completely from the people, places, possessions, and projects that make their lives meaningful and underpin their identities."[8] Preach it, Sue!

One of David's PCS moves took him to the village of Ziklag to escape the jealous wrath of King Saul. While there, he went on a raiding party to another village. When he returned he found that his enemies had burned Ziklag and had taken captive the women and children. In anger and grief, he and his men wept to the point of exhaustion. David's men took their grief to the extreme and wanted to stone him. David's identity went from hero to villain.[9] Nothing about his circumstances was encouraging.

The time in Ziklag was one of the greatest crises David faced. Sister, don't miss how David dealt with this emotional logistic: "He strengthened himself in the LORD."

He did not turn to other sources to numb his pain. He did not have supporting agencies from which to seek advice. Google search was not even a dream. However, he had a personal faith in God that could sustain him in the time of crisis.[10] I am thankful for the multiple resources available to provide help with my emotional logistics, but I am careful not to overlook the best resource to handle them: The Lord.

Respond

What PCS details cause you to become discouraged? In what ways you can strengthen yourself in the Lord?

Prayer for the journey

Lord, I cry to you for help. I know you will hear and deliver me out of all my troubles. You are near to the broken hearted and you save the crushed in spirit (Psalm 34:17–18).

Waypoint 6
A PCS playlist

The LORD will keep your going out and your coming
in from this time forth and forevermore. (Psalm 121:8)

Reflect

What is on your road trip playlist? Do you like to put the pedal
to the metal with rock anthems? Maybe you choose to let the
motor hum with classic country. Or, perhaps you prefer to
navigate your way with a little road-trip worship. If you choose
the latter, you are in good and ancient company. Jewish tradition
holds that Psalms 120–134 were the "road-trip playlist" for those
traveling to worship in Jerusalem. These songs, known as the
Psalms of Ascent, prepared their hearts for worship at the
temple as they made their way up to Mt. Zion.[11]

If I created a playlist for my next PCS, it would be filled with
songs that speak of God's faithfulness. The songs would point
my thoughts to the promise held in one of the songs sung by
ancient travelers in Psalm 121:3, "He will not let your foot be
moved; he who keeps you will not slumber."

I remember our PCS from Kansas to North Carolina. My
husband was in a car with one son, and I was in a second car
with another son. Of course, we were loaded down like the
Beverly Hillbillies and my husband was guiding our two-vehicle
caravan. Suddenly, the sprinkles of rain that were falling became
a torrential downpour. I could not see anything in front of me. I
did not have a cell phone to let my husband know I had stopped.
The fear of sliding off the road or of missing a turn he might
make was tangible.

At that moment, I did what any mom would do—I pulled off the road, grabbed my son's hand, and desperately prayed for God's help. After a while, the storm finally passed. I caught up with my husband who had been waiting for us a few miles down the road, and we were on our way again.

You know, I faced some other storms during that PCS—storms that did not bring rain—but tears. However, my experiences taught me that regardless of the nature of the storm, the nature of God is to keep me safe. He is a faithful traveling companion.

Respond

What are some songs that would be on your PCS playlist? How has God been a faithful traveling companion during your PCS seasons?

Prayer for the journey

Lord, my help comes from you. Remind me that you will keep me in my *going out and coming in*. Make my trust in you strong and confident. Amen.

Waypoint 7
Church shopping

Read

I was glad when they said to me, "Let us go to the house of the LORD!" (Psalm 122:1)

Reflect

While finding the right church is high on my PCS checklist, it can sometimes be like finding the right dress for an important occasion. I can look in ALL the shops, try on as many as possible, narrow it down to a few, and finally take one home wondering if the one left in the store was really the best one for me. There must be a better way to find a church!

For those who sang this Psalm of Ascent (Psalm 122)— there was only one house of God, and getting there was a difficult task for many of them. Although the trip to Jerusalem was demanding, the spiritual meaning and personal significance of God's house was so important that they joyfully made the journey. Jerusalem was where they experienced the joy shared as the community of God. At the house of the Lord, there was the special opportunity to worship the name of the Lord in his presence. Today as Christians who believe God is present everywhere, we can undervalue a moment of special encounter with God in corporate worship.[12]

Quickly locating and connecting with a local church is important to our relationship with God. Spiritual development as an individual and as a family can flounder if you finally find a church about the same time you get your next set of PCS orders.

In your plan for finding a church or military chapel, you may want to consider the following suggestions:

Pray for guidance. God may want you at a specific congregation for a purpose.

Do a digital recon of church websites to find out what a church believes; learn about their structure of worship or type of liturgy, leadership, and programs to fit your family, and their community involvement.

If you are a member of a specific denomination, check with your denominational headquarters for churches in your area. Identifying a church's denomination simply by the name on the sign is getting harder to do.

Remember there are many good churches, but there is no perfect church. You probably have heard the quip, "If I were to find a perfect church, it would lose that status when I joined." Don't just try to determine if the church is right for you, but also ask yourself: "Am I right for this church?"

Respond

What challenges have you had in finding a church home after a PCS? God created you with gifts meant to be shared within the body of Christ. How do you actively search for a place to share your unique gifts?

Prayer for the journey

Lord, thank you for the body of Christ. Fulfill your purpose in me and may my acts of service be faith-filled through your power. Amen.

Waypoint 8

Do good

Read

Do good, O LORD, to those who are good, and to those who are upright in their hearts! (Psalm 125:4)

Reflect

When you receive PCS orders, some decisions are best made after you arrive at your new location. You should wait until you can measure the windows before you order new curtains. Do not order checks with a new address until you have moved into your home. However, there is one thing you can certainly decide before your new military unit welcomes your family: *you can determine to do good.*

The travelers journeying to Jerusalem used this Psalm of Ascent (Psalm 125) to remind themselves that God blesses those who *do good.* Jesus taught on the virtues of doing good, even to those who do not deserve it (Luke 6:27–32). The apostle Paul emphasized that God created us in Christ to do good works (Ephesians 2:10). The Bible affirms that doing good brings glory to God (1 Peter 2:12). Doing good is so powerful it can even be the reason someone decides to become a Christian (1 Peter 3:1).

As a new person in town, you may be tempted to hide away and lay low until someone invites *(or drags)* you to a spouses' meeting or chapel event. However, doing good normally cannot be done in a social vacuum; it requires someone on the receiving end. Set a goal to *do good* in your new community as quickly as you can. You can get ready to do good at your new location before you arrive by practicing the following phrases to be used when you arrive:

"How can I help?"
"Is there anything you need?"
"When can I start?"

Doing good begins with the right frame of mind—having an upright heart, as the psalmist notes. The status of the heart clarifies that God is looking for more than just good deeds.[13] Our good deeds are to originate in a good heart. We do not earn our salvation by *doing good*, but we validate the good work the Lord has done in our hearts by the good work of our hands.

Respond

What does it mean for you to *do good*? What strategies have you used to help you get involved quickly at a new military assignment?

Prayer for the journey

Lord, remind me to do good today. Keep me focused on others and not on myself. Help me to meet people wherever they have a need, just as you have met me. Amen.

Waypoint 9
Twenty-eight years in rehab

O Lord, my heart is not lifted up;
    my eyes are not raised too high;
I do not occupy myself with things
    too great and too marvelous for me.
But I have calmed and quieted my soul,
    like a weaned child with its mother;
    like a weaned child is my soul within me
O Israel, hope in the Lord
    from this time forth and forevermore. (Psalm 131)

Reflect

Hello, my name is Brenda and I am a recovering control freak.

I spent twenty-eight years in rehab, otherwise known as "military life." God used military life to teach me the importance of relinquishing control. The most intense lesson always came when PCS orders arrived. Uncle Sam did not allow me to have any control over when those orders would arrive or where they would take our family.

When my husband received orders for Korea, I wondered whom he had angered. Korea was not on my list of places to visit, let alone live. The order to report within thirty days only increased the tension of the situation. Thirty days! He went to the military housing office to schedule the move, but there were no appointments available for several weeks. What did he do? My resourceful (i.e., desperate) soldier planted himself in the office and waited for an appointment no-show so he could get the ball rolling for our international move.

My husband's desire to calmly take care of his family was tossed in the air due to a hurried report date. Military life teaches you (if you are willing to learn) that when you do not have control of a situation, you respond the best way you can.

As a Christ follower, the *best way I can* would not mean trusting in my ability to control *my* circumstances, but would mean trusting in God who is over *all* circumstances. I long to learn the "tranquility of mature rest" described in Psalm 131.[14]

The message of Psalm 131 is the call to give less attention to my desires and efforts, and more to God's ordering of the issues of my life.[15] The psalm refers to the immature child who wants control. She wants to nurse when she wants to nurse. If you are a mom, you know that weaning a child is difficult. Crying and feelings of abandonment accompany the process, but the process is necessary for the child to mature. The process yields a weaned child who is content to rest beside mother, knowing mother will meet and provide for the needs.

Respond

Psalm 131:2 in *The Message* reads:
> *I've kept my feet on the ground,*
> *I've cultivated a quiet heart.*
> *Like a baby content in its mother's arms,*
> *My soul is a baby content.*

What does being content look like for you? What are ways you can cultivate "a quiet heart?"

Prayer for the journey

Lord, help me learn in whatever situation I am to be content. In any and every circumstance, help me learn the secret of facing plenty and hunger, abundance and need (Philippians 4:11–12). Amen.

Waypoint 10
Deferred travel

Behold, how good and pleasant it is, when brothers
dwell in unity! (Psalm 133:1)

When asked to share their best PCS advice, my friend Malinda
reported her husband's response: "Deferred travel!"

Deferred travel means the service member travels to the next
duty station, and the family follows later. My friend's response
was probably a tongue-in-cheek one. Malinda's husband could
make the argument that he would go to the next duty station
ahead of her in order to scope out the living conditions, get
comfortable in his new assignment, and learn his way around
their new town to better introduce it to his family. The unsaid
argument of course is, "I will go ahead and let *you* take care of
moving with the kids."

Deferred travel actually worked for us for several PCS
moves. When we moved to Germany, traveling alone with two
preschool children to meet my confident soldier on the other
side of the ocean was best. Our delayed arrival gave him the
opportunity to acclimate to his job and the new culture without
worrying about his family. Our transition overseas was much
easier. The plan worked well enough that we did it again when
we moved to Korea years later.

A PCS move is a prime opportunity to challenge the concept
of dwelling together in unity. The pilgrims traveling to Jerusalem
needed the reminder as they journeyed together. In the context
of Psalm 133, traveling in a group would generate plenty of

opportunity for tensions to simmer. Competition for resources, supplies, and dwelling en route provided potential for conflict among families and tribes.[16] The song they sang reminded them of the importance of traveling in harmony with one another. The unity they displayed as families would positively affect the entire nation.[17]

My sister in Christ, unity is a testimony to the world of the reality of Christ and will convince people that you have something they do not.[18] Jesus spoke of this unity in a prayer for his followers—"I in them and you in me. So that they may be brought to complete unity. Then the world will know that you sent me and have loved them even as you have loved me" (John 17:23 NIV).

Respond

What are the triggers that cause disunity in your family during a PCS move? How can you prepare to combat disunity during a PCS move?

Prayer for the journey

Lord, I pray our family would treat each other "with all humility and gentleness, with patience, bearing with one another in love, eager to maintain the unity of the Spirit in the bond of peace" (Ephesians 4:2–3). Amen.

Waypoint 11

On fire!

Read

Now Elijah the Tishbite, of Tishbe in Gilead, said to Ahab, "As the LORD, the God of Israel, lives, before whom I stand, there shall be neither dew nor rain these years, except by my word." (1 Kings 17:1)

Reflect

When you receive PCS orders to move to another nation, you become, in some ways, an ambassador for the United States. If you are a Christ follower, wherever you go, you are an ambassador for Christ. Chapter 17 of the book of 1 Kings introduces us to one of the more colorful personalities in Scripture, Elijah. His name means, "whose God is the Lord," or "my God is Yahweh." Elijah comes on the scene abruptly with no clear information about where he was born, his family history, or his education or training. We know he was a powerful man of God who took his marching orders directly from the Lord—and he moved around *a lot*.

Elijah was anything but a stoic, stuffy theologian. He engaged with the political and religious environment of his day and was bold to declare that he stood on the side of the Lord. As we look closely at some of Elijah's moves, we will see various responses that reveal his attitude toward each move. Just as PCS moves can bring out the best and worst in us, Elijah displayed a spectrum of emotions and actions as he moved from place to place.

The admirable trait that Elijah consistently displayed was his commitment to live his life in service to the Lord. Whether he was calling down fire from heaven, or in desperate need of food and water to survive, he did not waver in his commitment to live out the meaning of his name—*my God is Yahweh.*

Christ-followers in the military have the opportunity to live like Elijah. Carrying the name of the Lord to places across our nation and around the world is a privilege that many will never have. This does not mean that Christ followers need to call down fire from heaven. However, we can let the fire of the Lord burn within our hearts to the extent that we draw others to the warmth of Christ's love heard in our words and seen in our lives.

Respond

In what ways have you carried the name of the Lord as you move from place to place? How "hot" is your fire for the Lord burning today?

Prayer for the journey

Lord, I pray you would use me as a witness for you. Make my love for you burn so bright that my actions and words draw people to you. I want to be a strong representative for you wherever my feet lead me today. Amen.

Waypoint 12
A new pair of shoes

And the word of the LORD came to him: "Depart from here and turn eastward and hide yourself by the brook Cherith, which is east of the Jordan. You shall drink from the brook, and I have commanded the ravens to feed you there." So he went and did according to the word of the LORD. He went and lived by the brook Cherith that is east of the Jordan. And the ravens brought him bread and meat in the morning, and bread and meat in the evening, and he drank from the brook. (1 Kings 17:2b-6)

While many of the basic trainees continually complained to the chaplain about the schedule and living conditions, one of the new recruits seemed happy all the time. He told my husband: "I can't remember when someone cooked me three hot meals a day! And the shoes they issued me are the first pair of brand new shoes I've ever had in my life!" The Army met his needs and he was content. His attitude was refreshing!

Elijah prophesied boldly to the wicked king of Israel: "There shall be neither dew nor rain these years, except by my word" (1 Kings 17:1b). His message was blunt, brief, and confident. The gods King Ahab worshipped represented nonsense and Elijah came on the scene to make known that the one true God tolerated no rival.[19]

Following this encounter, the Lord told Elijah to leave the area and move for a time to an isolated spot by a brook. There God protected Elijah from the wrath of the king, and he prepared him for what was to come. There is no record of Elijah questioning God about the orders, but who could blame him if he did?

When asked to share his best PCS advice, my friend Brian mischievously said, "Go kicking and screaming!" That has been me on more than one occasion. That would have been me if God had told me to go live by a brook that only flowed in the rainy season with the promise that untamed ravens would bring me food. It would take much restraint not to ask, "Seriously, Lord?"

Thankfully, Elijah was better at obeying God than I would have been, because he did as God instructed. Beside that brook, God met all of Elijah's basic needs. You know, the Lord used ravens to feed Elijah and he has used Uncle Sam to feed my family and me. Sure, God can use General Motors, Wal-Mart, or any other company to provide for a family, but the military is one institution the Lord uses to meet the needs of some people. If you are reading this, chances are God is using the military to meet your needs.

Next time I move, I am confident the Lord will provide a place to live, food to eat, and if I need them, I can even buy myself a new pair of shoes!

Respond

How has God used the military to meet your needs? Take some time to list the ways you and your family's needs are met by the military.

Prayer for the journey

Lord, thank you for meeting my needs through my husband's military service. Forgive me when I express more complaints than gratitude. Remind me of the blessings that are mine and make me truly grateful. Amen.

Waypoint 13
Come live in our basement

Read

And after a while the brook dried up, because there was no rain in the land. Then the word of the LORD came to him, "Arise, go to Zarephath, which belongs to Sidon, and dwell there. Behold, I have commanded a widow there to feed you." (1 Kings 17:7–9)

Reflect

When the stream where Elijah was living dried up, the Lord ordered him to PCS to Zarephath in Sidon. This city was located in the heart of the pagan territory of Jezebel, wife of King Ahab of Israel.[20] She and her husband both wanted to do Elijah harm. Now if I had been in Elijah's sandals, I might have requested a change to these orders. I would have questioned the wisdom of going to a place where *my* God was not *their* god and where the most powerful woman in Israel, who wanted my head in a basket, had influential relatives.

On top of that, God's orders contained a footnote that said a widow would be taking care of his basic needs. This was not a rich widow, but one who was down to her last handful of meal and cup of oil. In fact, her plan was to make one last loaf of bread for her son and herself and then to die. I would be hard pressed not to say again, "Seriously, Lord?"

The Lord continues to teach me not to question how he can work out his plans for my family. If there was one place my husband did not want to be assigned it was Washington, DC. When PCS orders came down for DC in the middle of my son's senior year of high school, I was not a happy camper. We might as well have been Elijah getting ready to move to a godforsaken land. After the fact, I can say DC was a great place to live.

Our biggest logistical obstacle was maintaining a household in North Carolina to allow my son to finish high school while my husband found an inexpensive place to stay in Northern Virginia. Have you checked the cost of housing in Northern Virginia? The words inexpensive and housing do not go together there. We had no idea how we would afford to maintain two households.

As always, God had a plan. Through the involvement of one of my friends, a couple we had never met opened the basement apartment in their home to my husband for the cost of utilities alone. The woman said that she had never had anyone live in her house, but she believed the Lord had spoken to her to offer the space to this man whom she did not know. He lived there for six months before the rest of the family arrived.

Sister, God can use a PCS move to meet the needs of your family in ways that you have not imagined. Sometimes God uses people who seem most unlikely. Trust the Lord to know where you are going and what you need in order to make the transition.

Respond

Have you questioned the Lord's timing for a PCS move? If so, why? What lessons did you learn as the plan unfolded?

Prayer for the journey

Lord, help me to trust your timing in my life today. Remind me that "for everything there is a season, and a time for every matter under heaven" (Ecclesiastes 3:1). Amen.

Waypoint 14

Won't you be my neighbor?

Read

After many days the word of the LORD came to Elijah, in the third year, saying, "Go, show yourself to Ahab, and I will send rain upon the earth." (1 Kings 18:1)

Reflect

After three years in Zarephath, moving orders came again for Elijah. This time his assignment took him to Samaria where he made an appearance before King Ahab. Read 1 Kings 18 to see how the Lord used Elijah here. God energized him as he prayed, "O LORD, God of Abraham, Isaac, and Israel, let it be known this day that you are God in Israel, and that I am your servant, and that I have done all these things at your word. Answer me, O LORD, answer me, that this people may know that you, O LORD, are God, and that you have turned their hearts back" (1 Kings 18:36b–37). At that moment, fire fell from heaven and consumed all that was on the altar. Shocked, the people who saw the spectacle declared, "The LORD, he is God: the LORD, he is God" (1 Kings 18:39b).

If fire from heaven were not enough, Elijah bowed again to pray—this time for rain. God answered this prayer as well and the rain that had not fallen for three years fell from the sky.

The apostle James wrote: "Elijah was a man with a nature like ours, and he prayed fervently that it might not rain, and for three years and six months it did not rain on the earth. Then he prayed again, and heaven gave rain, and the earth bore its fruit" (James 5:17–18). What good news! Yes, Elijah was God's prophet, but the message of James is that the same power of prayer that Elijah demonstrated is available to you and me![21]

I recall looking out the window of our little row house. Germany had been home for a few months and I was feeling isolated and lonely. I did not see how I could contribute to my military community as a stay-at-home mom. I spoke no German and had little hope to affect the foreign community in which I lived. One morning during my devotional time, I read an entry in Oswald Chambers's *My Utmost for His Highest* in which he writes,

> Your part in intercessory prayer is … to utilize the commonsense circumstances God puts you in, and the commonsense people He puts you amongst, by His providence, to bring them before God's throne and give the Spirit in you a chance to intercede for them.[22]

Though I could not be sure of the opportunities this assignment would bring, I knew one thing: God had moved me here and now he moved in my heart to pray for my neighbors.

Sister, you do not know how God will use you when you move to a new location. Will he ask you to be a leader? Will you start a neighborhood Bible study in your home? Will you play a significant role in your military spouse support group? You may not be certain of the specifics, but you can be certain God wants you to pray with power, just like Elijah.

Respond

How can the words of Oswald Chambers, above, help you when you consider a PCS move?

Prayer for the journey

Lord, one of the greatest gifts I can offer my neighbors is prayer. I pray you would bless them with health and protection. I pray you would provide for their needs and grant them peace. I pray their relationships would be healthy and strong. I pray they would know you and be strengthened in their faith. Use me as your hands and feet in every interaction with my neighbors. Amen.

Waypoint 15
Overcome and overwhelmed

Ahab told Jezebel all that Elijah had done, and how he had killed all the prophets with the sword. Then Jezebel sent a messenger to Elijah, saying, "So may the gods do to me and more also, if I do not make your life as the life of one of them by this time tomorrow." Then he was afraid, and he arose and ran for his life and came to Beersheba, which belongs to Judah, and left his servant there. But he himself went a day's journey into the wilderness and came and sat down under a broom tree. (1 Kings 19:1–4a)

Reflect

Have you ever lived in a place where you tried to do everything right and things still went wrong? You do family devotions with your kids and one still gets in trouble at school. You go to church and even attend Bible study but you still have a neighbor that criticizes you. Your husband works long hard hours and his boss is still intent on ending his career. If so, you can identify with Elijah. He took a bold stand for God and Jezebel swore an oath to kill him within twenty-four hours. Yikes!

What do you do when things go wrong? Elijah may not have handled this one in the best possible way. He made an immediate unplanned move to the wilderness. To be more precise, the Scripture states, "He arose and ran for his life!"

Emotionally, fear overcame him—fear for his life. Healthy fear keeps us away from things that may harm us. Then there is crippling fear that shakes our confidence in ourselves, makes us question our faith in God, and moves us to go AWOL.

An immoral lifestyle in disobedience to God did not bring on Elijah's emotional state. God had sent him to the assignment where he confronted the evil rulers. Elijah was doing his best job. Yet his prophetic career had never faced such a tough challenge.

A time may come when you—or someone you know—find yourself struggling through a tough assignment. Your husband's job may be the source of the difficulty. The isolation of a difficult location may get you down. Problems with your children may seem overwhelming. Or, heaven forbid, you may face a combination of all three. If you find yourself ready to run—don't!

Jesus never said the life of a Christ follower would be easy. In fact, he warned us, "In the world you will have tribulation. But take heart, I have overcome the world" (John 16:33b).

The bad thing about a great assignment is that you have to leave in two or three years. The good thing about that place you can't wait to see in your rearview mirror is that you can leave in two or three years. The great thing about being a Christ follower is that he is with you always, in every place. When you are in a tough place, take heart in him.

Respond

What are some of the characteristics of a tough assignment? What hope do Psalm 3:4, Psalm 34:17, and Psalm 50:15 offer during overwhelming times?

Prayer for the journey

Lord, thank you for the assurance that you are with me always, in every place. Keep me in remembrance of this truth: "Blessed is the [woman] who remains steadfast under trial, for when [she] has stood the test [she] will receive the crown of life, which God has promised to those who love him" (James 1:12). Amen.

Waypoint 16
I've had enough!

Read

But he himself went a day's journey into the wilderness and came and sat down under a broom tree. And he asked that he might die, saying, "It is enough; now, O Lᴏʀᴅ, take away my life, for I am no better than my fathers." (1 Kings 19:4)

Reflect

"A whopping 90 percent of female military spouses—more than 600,000 people—are either unemployed or underemployed, according to a recent study,"[23] reported ABC News on a study by Syracuse University and the Institute for Veterans and Military Families. The study cited frequent moves as the leading cause of difficulty in military spouses finding employment.[24]

When you consider that what we do is closely associated with our assessment of who we are, you can understand how a military spouse can experience bouts of depression based on the repetitive cycle of reestablishing identity. This can be especially true when it comes to employment and career path. Military wife and journalist Michelle Aikman expressed it this way: "All of the momentum created before a move feels swept away—mobility can leave us feeling defeated and questioning our worth because we have to constantly prove it to gain access to new opportunities."[25]

Elijah followed up his fear of Jezebel's threats with an overwhelming sense of failure. He quit. He walked away from his assignment where thousands of people had seen him call down fire from heaven. He took off on a journey unsanctioned by God, and now he was alone in the desert, feeling like a failure, overwhelmed, and ready to die.

Isn't it amazing how the status of his self-assessment changed quickly with the change of location from Mt. Carmel to the wilderness of Beersheba? Most of us do not face the same circumstances as Elijah did in feeling his life threatened, but we can perhaps relate to the stress of fear brought on by relocation. Elijah interpreted Jezebel's threat as the end of his ministry.[26]

Elijah might have responded differently if he had predicted Jezebel's response to his prophetic role. He still should have called down the fire, and given it his best effort. However, she caught him off guard with her proclaimed death sentence. He did not see that one coming!

One way for military wives to lessen the disappointment that can accompany a perceived depreciation of status brought on by a PCS is to anticipate the need for an adjustment period after moving. More importantly, military wives who want to work, or not, should never forget that their value as a person cannot be determined by salary or position. Measure true worth only by eternal standards.

Even though Elijah left his "job," God was not finished with him. God has a life plan for us all. Check with him for your next position.

Respond

"People with their minds set on you, you keep completely whole, steady on their feet, because they keep at it and don't quit" (Isaiah 26:3 MSG). How does this Scripture encourage and challenge you as you think about the future?

Prayer for the journey

Lord, in the midst of change and challenge, help me be steadfast in my faith in you. Keep me on the path of obedience and trust. Amen.

Waypoint 17
Breakfast in bed

And [Elijah] asked that he might die, saying, "It is enough; now, O LORD, take away my life, for I am no better than my fathers." And he lay down and slept under a broom tree. And behold, an angel touched him and said to him, "Arise and eat." And he looked, and behold, there was at his head a cake baked on hot stones and a jar of water. And he ate and drank and lay down again. And the angel of the LORD came again a second time and touched him and said, "Arise and eat, for the journey is too great for you." And he arose and ate and drank, and went in the strength of that food forty days and forty nights to Horeb, the mount of God. (1 Kings 19:4b-8)

Reflect

As much as I loved military life, there were times, like Elijah, I said to the Lord, "I've had enough!" No sooner had I adjusted to a new place than it was time to leave. Don't get me wrong, I knew military life was God's will for our family, but there were days of struggle to align with my heart what I knew in my head.

One of my "I've had enough" times happened during a PCS move that took place in January. Moving in the off-season brought unique challenges. Life at the new duty station was already in full swing. My kids had to start school mid-year and I felt like I had to insert myself into groups that already had their momentum and rhythm. The idea exhausted me. So, what did I do? I am not proud of this, but for several months I locked my door, pulled the shades, and floundered in my isolation. Taking time to rest following a PCS is a good thing, but I went beyond the rest boundary and found myself depressed. I sent my kids off to school and, most mornings, I went back to bed. Bed was safe.

While I want to follow Elijah's example in many ways, this is one way I wish I did not relate. Elijah isolated himself. He reached the wilderness out of energy and all alone after having left his servant in Beersheba (1 Kings 19:3). Sister, let me tell you, when the going gets tough it is not the time to travel alone.

Our good God did not leave Elijah alone. In fact, he sent an angel to provide sustenance. God was not finished with Elijah. The prophet needed physical and spiritual strength to continue the journey and fulfill God's purpose, and God provided just what he needed. God did not tell Elijah to run for his life— that was Elijah reacting to his circumstances.[27] But God gently reminded Elijah through the food he sent that he was a God who was present with him and who would provide for him.[28]

Did you notice that something more than protein and carbs fortified the food the Lord's angel fed Elijah? After a second serving, Elijah was able to embark on a journey lasting forty days and forty nights. God knows the fortified spiritual nourishment we need to get out of our bed of despair and hit the trail to the place he knows we need to be. Taste and see that the Lord is good!

Respond

How did God care for Elijah physically, emotionally, and spiritually? How do God's actions toward Elijah give you confidence when you think about a PCS move?

Prayer for the journey

Lord, you have made me with body, soul, and spirit. You care not only for my spiritual well-being, you also care for my emotional and physical well-being. Help me to use wisdom to rest when I am tired from the day's activities. May I rest in your strength. Amen.

Waypoint 18

I'm the only one left!

There he came to a cave and lodged in it. And behold, the word of the LORD came to him, and he said to him, "What are you doing here, Elijah?" He said, "I have been very jealous for the LORD, the God of hosts, For the people of Israel have forsaken your covenant, thrown down your altars, and killed your prophets with the sword, and I, even I only, am left, and they seek my life, to take it away." (1 Kings 19:9–10)

Reflect

Our first military assignment was rich in deep relationships and community. We thrived as a family as we embraced living on a military installation. The close-knit neighborhood and sense of family in our chapel was an ideal introduction to military life. Then, everyone left. Our dearest friends and closest neighbors all moved away at the same time. I felt abandoned, as if I were the only one who stayed behind.

The food God fed Elijah gave him strength to journey forty days and nights until he came to a cave at Mt. Horeb. God asked Elijah, "What are you doing here?" Elijah's response was that he had worked hard for the Lord, but it did not matter because everyone else had forsaken God. He felt he was the only one left, so it made no sense to continue. Elijah was practicing selective memory. He was far from the only person left who served God. Read 1 Kings 18 and you will see one hundred prophets hidden (1 Kings 18:4), the people who seized the prophets of

Baal and killed them (1 Kings 18:40), and seven thousand godly worshippers in Israel! No, Elijah was not the only one left.[29]

I certainly can see how Elijah felt alone. That first assignment threw me a curve-ball in that I, too, felt as if I were the only one left. I knew it was not true, but it took time to grieve the departure of so many dear friends. I remembered how it felt to be the new military wife in the community two years earlier. I determined to look for opportunities to welcome new neighbors and new spouses to my husband's unit.

The fluidity of people coming and going let me see that I needed to be a productive part of a military community. The military tradition called the Hail and Farewell showed me the flow of time in being welcomed and in being welcoming. Whether in a formal setting or a family barbecue with your new unit, a Hail and Farewell introduces new members to the group as well as says goodbye to those leaving. So, when you are feeling down due to sad farewells, just look around and you will find someone who needs a warm hail. No matter how you feel, you are not alone.

Respond

How can you keep your witness for Christ bold and strong in the midst of a PCS move? What do Hebrews 13:5, Proverbs 18:1, Psalm 73:23, and Psalm 23:4 tell you about being or feeling alone?

Prayer for the journey

Lord, thank you for the promise never to leave or forsake me. May I always desire your presence and say: "But for me it is good to be near God; I have made the Lord God my refuge, that I may tell of all your works" (Psalm 73:28). Amen.

Waypoint 19

What are you doing here?

Read

And he said, "Go out and stand on the mount before the LORD." And behold, the LORD passed by, and a great and strong wind tore the mountains and broke in pieces the rocks before the LORD, but the LORD was not in the wind. And after the wind an earthquake, but the LORD was not in the earthquake. And after the earthquake a fire, but the LORD was not in the fire. And after the fire the sound of a low whisper. And when Elijah heard it, he wrapped his face in his cloak and went out and stood at the entrance of the cave. And behold, there came a voice to him and said, "What are you doing here Elijah?" (1 Kings 19:11–13)

Reflect

The assignment I mentioned earlier, during which I isolated myself, could have turned out differently. I often wonder what would have happened if I had stayed stuck in my melancholy. Looking back, I realize that was a turning point. My husband had been in the military long enough for me to see the potential for resentment to build up toward Uncle Sam. I had met military spouses who were bitter, angry, and hardened by military life. They looked backward in disappointment instead of forward in hope.

That PCS had brought me to a crossroads where I made a decision. I was not going to give up on hopeful possibilities nor give in to negative emotions. God had brought me to a place where I could hear his voice and he gently reminded me that this was the life to which he had called my family. I did not immediately feel positive about my circumstances, but I decided it was time to take a step toward building relationships and being involved in the community. I did not want to miss what I was to learn or how I was to serve.

1 Kings 19:11–13 reports Elijah moving to a new location, Mt. Horeb, also known as Mt. Sinai. This was the same place Moses first encountered God in the burning bush and later received the Ten Commandments from the Lord. He felt alone, but Elijah was not the first one to stand on this mountain before the Lord. When we think we struggle alone, we just need to look around to see the footprints left by many who have stood in the same dust of despair. Human struggle is not unique.

On Mt. Horeb, God repeated the question to Elijah, "What are you doing here?" Like a wise counselor, God was asking him to do some soul-searching and re-evaluation of his circumstances. He allowed Elijah to vent his frustrations and he listened patiently. We often look for the miraculous and the spectacular as the only way God can speak and show himself. But God's message to Elijah is a message to you and me. He is sometimes in the quiet moments of change, the times of waiting, and yes, even the times of disappointment.

God knew Elijah was at a difficult place. I find it encouraging that God did not leave Elijah on a mountain with questions echoing through the caverns of his heart. The Lord redirected his focus and got him moving in the right direction. Sister, God will not leave you when you are confused and discouraged. He wants to engage and redirect us. He cares and he has a purpose.

Respond
How can a PCS move keep you from hearing the "low whispers" of God? What can you do to help you hear God's whispers?

Prayer for the journey
Lord, make my ears quick to listen to your voice. Still my heart today and let me know you are God. Amen.

Waypoint 20
#Listersgottalist

Read

And the LORD said to him, "Go, return on your way to the wilderness of Damascus. And when you arrive, you shall anoint Hazael to be king over Syria. And Jehu the son of Nimshi you shall anoint to be king over Israel, and Elisha the son of Shaphat of Abel-meholah you shall anoint to be prophet in your place. (1 Kings 19:15–16)

Reflect

The "#listersgottalist" tag line on Instagram got my attention. After a little digging, I discovered a huge group of folks who have made a hobby out of creative listing. The concept is to create lists about things you love, goals you want to achieve, and memories you want to keep by creating a decorative journal filled with lists. Over twenty thousand people have downloaded the journal prompts and accepted the creative list challenge.

I admire anything that facilitates creativity and promotes goal-setting and memory-keeping. My list-making efforts tend to be more practical. I would hate to admit how many times I get home from the grocery store only to realize I did not purchase the very thing that prompted me to shop! Yes, I need a list to keep me on track.

We've mentioned before the helpful nature of lists during a PCS. When you are under the type of stress brought on by a PCS, forgetting important details is easy.

Elijah was under stress, but what did God do? He gave him a list of what to do next. Elijah did not have to think deeply or be in a super-spiritual state of mind. He just had to follow the checklist. The tasks focused his energy on something other than his circumstances.

Elijah did not respond with renewed strength or vigor, but he did take a step in the right direction. He functioned and moved forward to journey to three different places and accomplish three critical tasks. He put into practice the adage for success: "function whether you feel like it or not."

During a PCS, we do not always have to do everything with excitement and enthusiasm. We just need a good list of what we need to do, and then, like the Nike motto implores us—just do it!

Respond
What are the benefits of acting on the advice to "function whether you feel like it or not"? Be a "lister" and make a list of the things you need to do today. Take the details of your day to God in prayer.

Prayer for the journey
Lord, grant me the strength to accomplish the tasks set before me today. Help me "fix [my] eyes not on what is seen, but on what is unseen, since what is seen is temporary, but what is unseen is eternal" (2 Corinthians 4:18 NIV). Amen.

Waypoint 21

A lot!

Not that I am speaking of being in need, for I have learned in whatever situation I am to be content. (Philippians 4:11)

Reflect

In how many cities have you lived? Into how many homes have you moved? How many times have you received PCS orders?

Numbers do not stay in my head, so when I'm asked the questions above I usually respond with, "A lot!" I connect the years we lived in a place not by dates, but by the age of my children at the time. My ineptness with numbers is embarrassing and is one of the reasons I trained to be a kindergarten teacher. The point is, as a military wife, I moved *a lot*, and I have lived in *a lot* of different houses.

The life Scripture of a military wife could easily be the American Standard Version of Philippians 4:11: "Not that I speak in respect of want: for I have learned, in whatsoever state I am, therein to be content." Yes, whether the state was North Carolina (twice), Georgia (twice), Virginia (twice), Pennsylvania, New Jersey, Kansas, or even beyond our U.S. states to Germany and Korea, I learned to be content. PCS moves can only be successful if you learn to find satisfaction "in whatsoever state" you find yourself.

The apostle Paul did his share of moving from place to place as well. In how many cities did God assign him to work? *A lot*. He was the one who wrote Philippians 4:11 on the topic of contentment—from prison—while awaiting a possible death sentence!

Paul continues in Philippians 4:12–13, "I know how to be brought low, and I know how to abound. In any and every circumstance, I have learned the secret of facing plenty and hunger, abundance and need. I can do all things through him who strengthens me."

People are prone to misuse Paul's words as a biblical magic lamp to rub and have "all things" made better. That would make God a magic genie who instantly wipes out difficulties. In *The Most Misused Verses in the Bible,* Eric Bargerhuff writes that Philippians 4:13 "is about having strength to be content when we are facing those moments in life when physical resources are minimal."[30] PCS season brings with it *a lot* of stress, *a lot* of confusion, *a lot* of frustration, and *a lot* of weariness. Paul's message in Philippians 4:11–13 is that God is a sustainer when life brings us *a lot* of challenges.

Over the next few days, we will trace some of Paul's journeys and the challenges he faced. One thing I can guarantee we will discover is that wherever Paul went God had something special in store for him. Sister, wherever *you* go the Lord has something special in store for you. He wants to use you—a lot—even through the challenges of a PCS.

Respond
Notice the key word *learned* in Philippians 4:11. What has military relocation taught you about contentment? In what ways do you struggle to find contentment in relation to military PCS?

Prayer for the journey
Lord, forgive me when desires overwhelm my heart. Give me a teachable spirit that I may apply your Word and be content in every situation. Fill my heart with your peace when I become anxious. Amen.

Waypoint 22

A traveling testimony

When they had gone through the whole island as far as Paphos, they came upon a certain magician, a Jewish false prophet named Bar-Jesus. He was with the pro-consul, Sergius Paulus, a man of intelligence, who summoned Barnabas and Saul and sought to hear the word of God. But Elymas the magician (for that is the meaning of his name) opposed them, seeking to turn the proconsul away from the faith. But Saul, who was also called Paul, filled with the Holy Spirit, looked intently at him and said, "You son of the devil, you enemy of all righteousness, full of all deceit and villainy, will you not stop making crooked the straight paths of the Lord? And now, behold, the hand of the Lord is upon you, and you will be blind and unable to see the sun for a time." Immediately mist and darkness fell upon him, and he went about seeking people to lead him by the hand. Then the proconsul believed, when he saw what had occurred, for he was astonished at the teaching of the Lord. (Acts 13:6–12)

Reflect

Every major U.S. military headquarters has a mission to engage with military leaders from other nations. When units are stationed OCONUS (Outside the Continental United States), American units commonly have a connection with a sister unit from the host nation. In addition to the formal military and political discussions between the organizations, informal exchanges and sharing take place covering social customs, sports—and religion.

Paul, Barnabas, and a team journeyed to Cyprus, an island a bit smaller than Connecticut. In the city of Paphos they met Sergius Paulus, the Roman official over the province. The Scripture states that he was an intelligent man and wanted to hear Paul and Barnabas talk about the Word of God.

We have lived in a few places where my husband had the opportunity to talk about faith with other military personnel. During one foreign exchange training exercise, a Muslim officer sought out my husband at a social outing and spent several hours in discussion about my husband's faith in Christ. One neighbor in Germany declared herself an agnostic, yet she had many questions about my faith and gave me the opportunity to share my story. In Korea I had many invitations to talk with Korean women, most of whom were Buddhists, about American culture, which, for me, included my faith in Christ. Each assignment holds unique opportunities to share your faith—not in what is called cold-turkey Bible-banging, but in conversation with those, like Serguis Paulus, who have a genuine interest in the faith they see in you.

We don't know the degree of Sergius Paulus's belief.[31] Likewise, we may never know the level of our life's influence on others, but we can be confident that the Spirit can use our words and testimony to facilitate an eternal change in someone's life.

Respond

Have you had an opportunity to share your experience with Jesus? Describe the moment. If you have never shared your testimony, write it down in your journal so you will be ready when the opportunity comes. You can find a worksheet to help you at: cru.org/train-and-grow/how-to-tell-your-story-worksheet.html

Prayer for the journey

Lord, open a door for me to declare the mystery of Christ. You've brought me to this place to be a light for you. Give me clarity to share the story of my salvation. Amen.

Waypoint 23
Who knows?

Now Paul and his companions set sail from Paphos and came to Perga in Pamphylia. And John left them and returned to Jerusalem. (Acts 13:13)

Reflect

Later in your life you will probably reflect on your military assignments and realize they were less about place and more about people. BRAC (Base Closure and Realignment Commission) might shut down an installation where you had fond memories of living in historic government quarters. You might take a personal trip to Europe only to have trouble finding the fenced compound on which you lived because it has been converted to a local neighborhood with new apartment buildings and businesses. But bulldozers cannot take from you the memories and relationships with people you met there.

Not all our memories of people are fond. In fact, some initial encounters can make you wish there were such a thing as a human bulldozer to move them out of the way. Paul's response to John Mark likely fell into this category as John abruptly left the team at Perga. The Scripture passage does not state why John Mark left, but Paul did not find his reason to be acceptable. In fact, Paul had such strong negative feelings about him that he refused to allow John Mark to travel with him on the next missionary journey. Barnabas wanted to take John Mark, but you can almost hear Paul responding with an insistent tone, "Remember Perga?"

When moving to a new location, getting everything set up takes work. Sometimes my husband has to move the couch to all four walls of the living room before I decide which location is best. Energy and effort always go into getting my children settled in the right classes and groups. Likewise, most new friendships do not come easy. At first encounter, you may not foresee a close friendship with a new acquaintance. The possibility exists that a first encounter may even be negative to the point that you do not want that person around, just like Paul felt about John Mark.

But don't be too quick to permanently write someone off your potential friend list. If you stay in the military long enough, there is a chance you will run across them again. People can change. You and I can change. Relationships can change.

In fact, if you do further investigation into the relationship—maybe non-relationship would be a better description—between Paul and John Mark, you will find an interesting twist. Near the end of Paul's life, while confined to prison in Rome awaiting a likely death sentence, he sent for John Mark.[32] Considering Paul's circumstances, why would he call for John Mark? Obviously, their relationship had changed over the years, and for the better. In asking for John Mark, Paul told Timothy, "He is very useful to me for ministry" (2 Timothy 4:11).

Who knows whom you will meet during your next assignment? Who knows with whom you will easily hit it off and with whom you won't? Who knows who will end up being a friend for life?

Respond
Have you ever been quick to write someone off your potential friend list? Describe the situation. What does the change in Paul's attitude toward John Mark teach you about friendship?

Prayer for the journey
Lord, help me be humble, gentle, and patient, bearing with others in love, as I make every effort to keep the unity of the Spirit in the bond of peace. Amen. (See Ephesians 4:2–3.)

Waypoint 24
Move forward

Read

After the reading from the Law and the Prophets, the rulers of the synagogue sent a message to them, saying, "Brothers, if you have any word of encouragement for the people, say it." (Acts 13:15)

Reflect

The assignment was a town called Antioch in Pisidia. Paul and Barnabas went to the local synagogue for worship. The leader recognized Paul and Barnabas as visitors and, according to custom, gave them an opportunity to speak.[33] Paul accepted the invitation and began to talk about Jesus in the context of historical Judaism. After what was evidently an eloquent and interesting presentation, the congregation begged Paul and Barnabas to come back the next week and talk more about Jesus.

By the next week, word of mouth caused almost the whole town to show up (Acts 13:44). Then it happened. The Jews became so jealous of the crowds that they began to contradict and bad-mouth Paul (Acts 13:45). When the Jews rejected the message, Paul took the message of Jesus to the non-Jews. The Gentiles were receptive to the gospel and many became Christ-followers. The good news spread throughout the region. This got under the skin of the Jews and they stirred up the city leaders to persecute Paul and Barnabas and run them out of town (Acts 13:50).

What lessons can we learn from Paul's experience for when we move to a new place and make an effort to get involved? First, religious people normally invite newcomers to participate in their group. But if you are more successful than those in charge, you might encounter jealousy. Third, jealousy can cause people to act rudely toward those they feel are encroaching on their territory.

Can this happen among Christians in a church or chapel? Only if humans make up the group. Even humans saved by grace can be distrustful of anything (or anyone) new. When you are the new person, get to know others before you show everyone a better way to do things. When you are the one offering welcome, be open to the gifts God has given others and practice hospitality.

Note Paul's response: "But they shook off the dust from their feet against them and went to Iconium" (Acts 13:51). Jesus used this phrase in Matthew 10:14. The act symbolized ridding oneself of impurities picked up from walking through the land of those who would not believe.[34] Sister, when you meet rejection or distrust after reaching out, don't allow resentment, offense, or defeat to settle in your soul. Beware the "why try?" syndrome.

In her wonderful book, *After the Boxes are Unpacked*, my friend Susan Miller writes:

To let go allows God to mend you.
To start over allows God to mold you.
To move forward allows God to mature you.[35]

Paul and his team did not let rejection keep them down. They kept moving forward, joyously: "And the disciples were filled with joy and with the Holy Spirit" (Acts 13:52). Move forward in joy today, my friend!

Respond
In what ways have you let a lukewarm reception or rejection keep you from becoming involved after a PCS? Is God asking you to let go, start over, or move forward?

Prayer for the journey
Lord, keep me from childish thoughts. Help me to cooperate with the process of spiritual maturity and be filled with joy today. Amen.

Waypoint 25

'Cause your friends are my friends

Read

Paul came also to Derbe and to Lystra. A disciple was there, named Timothy, the son of a Jewish woman who was a believer, but his father was a Greek. He was well spoken of by the brothers at Lystra and Iconium. Paul wanted Timothy to accompany him ..." (Acts 16:1–3a)

To Timothy, my true child in the faith ...
(1 Timothy 1:2a)

Reflect

The more we get together, together, together,
The more we get together, the happier we'll be.
'Cause your friends are my friends,
and my friends are your friends.
The more we get together, the happier we'll be.

The lyrics of this children's song remind me of military friendships. Often when our family moved to a new duty station, I had names of people to call, or someone had been given my name to call me upon arrival.

Friends of friends became my friends. When I met Susan, I did not know if we would have anything in common. We seemed very different. However, she was a good friend of my friend Ruth, so I thought chances were that Susan and I could become good friends as well. I was right! Susan became, and remains, a great friend. We found that we had much in common and Susan is someone with whom I do not allow too much time to pass before making a connection.

Paul's journey to Derbe and Lystra put him in contact with a young man named Timothy. Scripture informs us that Timothy's reputation preceded him, no doubt because he had friends in adjoining communities.[36] Paul heard about him through his friends and wanted to take him along on his journey.[37]

Paul mentions Timothy several times throughout his writings. Two books of the New Testament are letters Paul wrote to Timothy. Over time, Timothy became like family to Paul. Paul addresses him as "my child," a close and intimate term of endearment. Theirs was a relationship grounded in their common faith in Christ.[38]

You do not know which assignment will bring friends who will eventually become like family. The song is true though, "The more we get together, the happier we'll be."

Respond

Make a list or graph of some of the friendships that military life has brought you. What does Paul pray for the believers in Colossians 1:9–12?

Prayer for the journey

(Use the list you wrote from Colossians 1:9–12 as a guide to pray for your friends today.)

Waypoint 26
Orders in hand

And when they had come up to Mysia, they attempted to go into Bithynia, but the Spirit of Jesus did not allow them. So, passing by Mysia, they went down to Troas. (Acts 16:7–8)

Reflect

"Have you signed a contract on a house yet?" were the words my husband heard from the assignment officer on the other end of the line. With orders in hand, we had just spent most of our Christmas leave at our next duty station looking at neighborhoods and houses for the upcoming move. This assignment was in a city where we were eager to relocate. My husband was looking forward to the job for which his new boss-to-be had handpicked him. Win-win, right?

You guessed it. A few phone conversations later and my husband's assignment was changed. We would be headed three states over to a totally unfamiliar environment and a yet-to-be-determined job for my husband.

At times like this, a number of questions run through a wife's mind, such as: "Who did my husband tick off?" or "Do assignment officers have a clue about what they are doing?" or "Does the military even care about what we want?"

Looking at today's Scripture focus, Paul may have had a few questions about where he wanted to go too. The Scripture states that Paul and team desired to go to Bithynia, but the Spirit of Jesus did not allow them. Whoa—assignment orders changed by Jesus himself? One would think that Paul ran every assignment by the Lord before hitting the road to the next place. The Scripture is not clear about that part, but what is clear is that the Spirit of Jesus changed Paul's next assignment.

If you are concerned about your next assignment, I have good news for you. First, God has a plan for you and knows where he wants you to be. Second, God knows how the assignment process works for each branch of service. Third, God can easily direct the mind of the key assignment person that writes your husband's orders.

By the way, the changed assignment I mentioned above ended up being one of the most crucial assignments for my husband's military career, and one of the most rewarding for my family and me. Trust God to direct your next assignment, even if your orders are changed!

Respond
What is your normal response to unexpected changes? What do you learn about flexibility from Philippians 4:12–13?

Prayer for the journey
Lord, help me to learn to trust your plan. Give me a flexible spirit that does not fight against revisions to *my* plan. Amen.

Waypoint 27

The interrogation room

About midnight Paul and Silas were praying and singing hymns to God, and the prisoners were listening to them, and suddenly there was a great earthquake, so that the foundations of the prison were shaken. And immediately all the doors were opened, and everyone's bonds were unfastened. When the jailer woke and saw that the prison doors were open, he drew his sword and was about to kill himself, supposing that the prisoners had escaped. But Paul cried with a loud voice, "Do not harm yourself, for we are all here." And the jailer called for lights and rushed in, and trembling with fear he fell down before Paul and Silas. Then he brought them out and said, "Sirs, what must I do to be saved?" And they said, "Believe in the Lord Jesus, and you will be saved, you and your household." (Acts 16:25–31).

Reflect

Our passports arrived. We were ready to join my husband in Korea. We knew this move would offer our family a unique view of Asian culture. Germany had felt far away from home, but now the move to Korea seemed like going to another planet. The long flight did nothing to dispel that opinion!

We landed and joined the line for Immigration Control. I handed over our passports. Two were stamped and then, while examining the third, the agent looked at me strangely—the kind of look you do *not* want to come your way in such a place. He said, "Step this way, ma'am." My boys and I were ushered into a small room. I had no idea what was happening. It felt like a bad spy movie. My imagination went wild as I sat and waited for the interrogation to begin. Korean officers entered the room with our passports in hand.

"Why are you in Korea?" "How long will you stay?" The questions went on. Eventually I learned that the passport for my youngest son lacked a status of forces agreement (SOFA) stamp. I had noticed the discrepancy when our passports arrived, but I concluded he was too young to need it. The military provided our passports and I assumed they were correct. Silly, silly me!

When Paul traveled he had certain rights as a Roman citizen, but the local authorities did not initially respect his rights. He was unlawfully beaten and thrown into jail. We were treated with respect and kindness in Korea, but we were still emotionally rattled. The authorities gave us a temporary entry stamp and assured us we could procure a permanent SOFA stamp from the embassy. The Lord knows how to help us even when red tape entangles our lives.

God worked things out for Paul and Silas as well. When the city officials learned that Paul was a Roman citizen, they came to his cell and personally apologized. Of greater importance was the conversion of the jailor and his family, which may not have happened if Paul had not been thrown in jail in the first place. Military dependents live under the laws of the homeland, and when assigned overseas, under the laws of a foreign land. More importantly, we live under the laws of the Lord. Sister, be encouraged, because God tends to rule in our favor.

Respond

Has red tape been an obstacle in any of your PCS moves? What keeps you from viewing such obstacles as opportunities?

Prayer for the journey

Lord, help me see myself as your representative wherever you lead me. Use me to share your love with others today. Amen.

Waypoint 28

Be a Berean

Read

The brothers immediately sent Paul and Silas away by night to Berea, and when they arrived they went into the Jewish synagogue. Now these Jews were more noble than those in Thessalonica; they received the word with all eagerness, examining the Scriptures daily to see if these things were so. (Acts 17:10–11)

Reflect

One of the unexpected blessings of military life for me has been the discovery of a unique women's ministry. Protestant Women of the Chapel (PWOC) is a military chapel sponsored ministry with the goals of leading women to Christ, teaching women the Word of God, developing spiritual gifts in women, and involving women in chapel ministry. My association with PWOC began during our first assignment, and many years later, the ties are still strong.

When our family arrived at each new duty station, one of the first things I did was search for a PWOC chapter. I knew I would find sisters in Christ who were eager to study God's Word. My deepest friendships were nurtured through participation in PWOC. Most importantly, my relationship with the Lord grew as women challenged me to go deeper with God. We dropped rank, ethnicity, and denominational differences at the door. Our common love for Jesus bound us together.

Paul's encounter with the Bereans reminds me of my encounter with PWOC. The Scripture passage describes this group as noble, eager, and committed. They were noble, not because of their birth, but because of their willingness to learn. Their willingness resulted in an eagerness to study God's Word and hear from him.[39] Paul arrived in Berea on the heels of some jealous Jews who wanted him out of Thessalonica.

On the one hand, it must have been refreshing to arrive in Berea and meet people who did not care about social status. On the other hand, they did not accept Paul's teaching without question. They tested and confirmed Paul's message with the Jewish Scriptures (Old Testament) and prophecies. The Bereans eagerly awaited the Messiah. When they heard Paul's message, they wanted to receive it but also made sure to verify his words.

Not every military installation is fortunate enough to sponsor a PWOC group, but wherever you go, commit yourself to living like a Berean. Make sure that what you read and what others teach you lines up with the Scriptures, and associate with those who have a hunger for God's Word.

Respond

How are you living like a Berean? How can studying God's Word with others help you adjust to a new duty station?

Prayer for the journey

Lord, increase my love for your Word. Give me a spirit of discernment to test the teaching I hear. Protect me from false teaching and foolish doctrine. Amen.

Waypoint 29
A fond farewell

Read
And when he had said these things, he knelt down and prayed with them all. And there was much weeping on the part of all; they embraced Paul and kissed him, being sorrowful most of all because of the word he had spoken, that they would not see his face again. And they accompanied him to the ship. (Acts 20:36–38)

Reflect

During a traditional military Hail and Farewell those being hailed are normally recognized but not given an opportunity to speak, whereas those who are leaving are often asked if they have anything to say. The same pattern is true for change of command ceremonies. Protocol offers the outgoing commander more freedom with the length of remarks, but the incoming commander is limited to a few succinct comments. Farewell remarks about shared events and actions can be emotional and heartfelt. An organization develops a special bond through both good times and difficult periods together.

In the verses immediately preceding today's reading (Acts 20:17–35), the apostle Paul bids farewell to a group of people for whom he cared deeply. He recounted the times of great success and recalled the events that brought tears. He assured them that the Spirit of God motivated all he did for them for their good. He expressed concern for their future and cautioned them to continue to faithfully follow the Lord. He shared with them what he believed to be the challenges awaiting him and asked for their prayers.

The farewell ended with tears, hugs, kisses, and prayers. An uninformed observer would have easily surmised that the people cared deeply about one another.

When we think about issues pertaining to a PCS, our thoughts focus mainly on the hail and not the eventual farewell. Here is a challenge: start mentally writing your farewell speech the day you arrive. By this, I mean be intentional about making a difference in people's lives. Along with your plans of where to go on leave and what to see and do over long weekends, look early on to determine whom you can encourage, where in the community you can help, and what role you can play in church or chapel.

If we approach a new assignment with the attitude of Paul— to serve others and follow the leading of God's Spirit, then our farewell memories will already be written in the hearts of those we come to know.

Respond
Spend time today writing a farewell speech you would like to give when you leave this assignment. What must be your priorities in order to be able to give your speech when you leave?

Prayer for the journey
Now to him who is able to keep me from stumbling and to present me blameless before the presence of his glory with great joy, to the only God, our Savior, through Jesus Christ our Lord, be glory, majesty, dominion, and authority, before all time and now and forever. Amen. (See Jude 24–25.)

Waypoint 30

Just show up!

And the brothers there, when they heard about us, came as far as the Forum of Appius and Three Taverns to meet us. On seeing them, Paul thanked God and took courage. (Acts 28:15)

Reflect

Our family has experienced arriving at a new duty station and receiving a warm welcome as well as arriving at a new duty station thinking that someone engraved "ignore me" on our foreheads. I prefer the warm welcome—what about you? All branches of military service put forth an effort to provide information to new residents, and the military as a whole has a welcoming culture.

The scene in Acts 28:15 describes Paul's arrival in Italy after a long and hazardous journey. A shipwreck, a snakebite, and a three-month unexpected layover in Malta were not on the original itinerary (Acts 27). The challenging trip made the welcome Paul received from the Jewish Christians in Rome even more special. Paul thanked God at the sight of these folks walking down the road. No one called them on a cell phone to let them know Paul arrived. They did not receive a telegram from sea to inform them the ship would be in port. The Holy Spirit sent them on their journey—over thirty miles!—at just the right time to give Paul the welcome of a dignitary.[40] They traveled the distance with no agenda but to show up and welcome him to the neighborhood.

The actions of the Roman Jews inspire me. I think of the times I made excuses to stay safe within my four walls. The effort to meet new people seemed overwhelming. I never think how my "showing up" might encourage someone else. Folks put great effort into planning newcomer gatherings, Bible studies, church services, spouse gatherings, and even information briefings. I tend to have a *selfie* attitude when I move—people are supposed to show up for me. What difference would it make if I turned the focus around?

Friend, no one may welcome you to your new duty station as if you were a dignitary. In fact, you too may feel like someone stamped "ignore me" on your forehead. May I encourage you to guard against making excuses that will keep you from showing up. Your presence could be just the encouragement someone else needs. Where will you *show up* today?

Respond
What are ways that people have made you feel welcome when you arrive in a new place? When has someone *showing up* made a difference in your life?

Prayer for the journey
Lord, thank you for the many times people have shown up and blessed me with their presence. Help me to be willing to show up for others and not discount the ministry of my presence in their lives. Amen.

Journey 2

Determined to Thrive in Transition

JOURNEY OF A MILITARY WIFE

Introduction

PCS moves are only one type of transition. In fact, transitions characterize all of life as they indicate movement. If you are a Christ-follower, transition is an opportunity to grow in your faith. However, transition can be awkward and unsettling, while at the same time present new challenges and choices to cooperate with God and draw closer to him.

Transitions may bring an end to a season, a situation, a relationship, or an attitude in order to begin anew. The sense of loss that accompanies transition is real and we must make time to grieve. The conflicting emotions are good and healthy. Saying goodbye makes way for saying hello to new seasons, new possibilities, new friends, and new hope! Much can happen during transition, and, between the place of change and acceptance, we can get stuck in the struggle to want everything settled—now! Taking the time to see God in the midst of the transition is important. Recognizing he is setting the pace, even when you cannot see him, is reassuring.

Walk with me on another thirty-day journey. Take steps toward peace in times of transition as you view the transitions of some heroes of the faith. Peter, Esther, Naomi, Ruth, Caleb, and Daniel all experienced extraordinary transitions that changed the trajectory of their lives toward God's purpose. We will also walk with the disciples on the Emmaus Road and relive Paul's dramatic Damascus Road encounter with Christ. Prayerfully, we will discover how to thrive through our own transitions. Do not forget to begin each day with the prayer from Psalm 119:18: Lord, "Open my eyes, that I may behold wondrous things out of your law."

You will find that the journey of transition is one expedition you don't want to miss!

Waypoint 1

Peter—A man in transition

Read

At Caesarea there was a man named Cornelius, a centurion of what was known as the Italian Cohort, a devout man who feared God with all his household, gave alms generously to the people, and prayed continually to God. About the ninth hour of the day he saw clearly in a vision an angel of God come in and say to him, "Cornelius." And he stared at him in terror and said, "What is it, Lord?" And he said to him, "Your prayers and your alms have ascended as a memorial before God. And now send men to Joppa and bring one Simon who is called Peter. He is lodging with one Simon, a tanner, whose house is by the sea." When the angel who spoke to him had departed, he called two of his servants and a devout soldier from among those who attended him, and having related everything to them, he sent them to Joppa. (Acts 10:1–8)

Reflect

What words come to mind when you think of *transition*? The common response is *change,* but these are not necessarily the same. In the book *Transitions* William H. Bridges suggests that change is an event while transition is a process. It's a valuable distinction. I see *change* as the events that occur in my life and *transition* as the process of adapting to those changes.

In today's reading, God is getting ready to make a big change in kingdom citizenship. Up to this point only believing Jews made up the church. The expectation for joining the Christ-followers was to commit to observe Jewish law *in addition* to following Christ. But change was coming. Gentiles would be welcomed without needing to follow Jewish rituals. Peter and the other believers would need to go through a major transition.

Peter was not ready for this, but change happens whether we want it or not: a PCS, a deployment, a new job, a new child, retirement. Our willing participation predicts how well we will transition—adjust emotionally and mentally to the change. I desire to thrive in transition, but my path from *functioning* to *thriving* is filled with potholes, curves, detours, and at times, complete standstills.

Tough transitions are not for the faint of heart. God picked the right person to walk with Peter on this journey. Cornelius was a soldier, a centurion in command of a hundred men, a Gentile. Did you get that? The man God picked to transition Peter through a big church change was a *soldier*—not a teacher, not a doctor, but a *soldier*. The first Gentile Christ-follower. Awesome!

God sent an angel instructing Cornelius to summon Peter. His response was to stare in terror! Do you blame him? He had faced battles, but this heavenly being was intimidating. And the angel's message gave no indication of the outcome if he obeyed.[1]

Fear is a natural response to the unknowns that accompany transition, to all that we cannot control or predict, especially regarding the welfare of our family. But to thrive in transition we must not freeze in fear of potential outcomes. Acknowledging fear is the first step in moving forward courageously.

Respond

What fears have you experienced in transition? What is outside your control now? Write your fears in a journal. Make them a prayer guide on your journey toward accepting change.

Prayer for the journey

Lord, you have not given me a spirit of fear but of power and love and a sound mind (2 Timothy 1:7). Help me walk through transition with peace that only comes as I trust in you. I lay these fears before you and ask you to help me overcome them today. Amen.

Waypoint 2
'No way!'

The next day, as they were on their journey and approaching the city, Peter went up on the housetop about the sixth hour to pray. And he became hungry and wanted something to eat, but while they were preparing it, he fell into a trance and saw the heavens opened and something like a great sheet descending, being let down by its four corners upon the earth. In it were all kinds of animals and reptiles and birds of the air. And there came a voice to him: "Rise, Peter; kill and eat." But Peter said, "By no means, Lord; for I have never eaten anything that is common or unclean." And the voice came to him again a second time, "What God has made clean, do not call common." This happened three times, and the thing was taken up at once to heaven. (Acts 10:9–16)

Reflect

What was this thing in my house? My airborne jumpmaster-wannabe husband had brought home a semblance of a mannequin strapped with a packed parachute. He said he had to practice the steps of inspecting a paratrooper's parachute. I watched him move his hands over the training aid while speaking military nomenclature aloud. He did this over and over and over. Military wives are accustomed to watching their husbands do repetitive processes for the purpose of precision.

In the incident with Peter, a voice accompanied his vision of a sheet that held all types of animals, reptiles, and birds descending to earth. The voice instructed Peter to kill and eat the animals not once, not twice, but three times. Unlike my husband in training, God did not repeat the vision three times for the purpose of precision, but for persuasion. The command to kill animals and eat them may seem like a no-brainer to our Western mindset. However, Jewish law prohibited Peter from eating meat that was not kosher. The command went against Peter's lifelong training and practice.[2] For the Jews, food restrictions were not about etiquette or being a picky eater. Adherence to the strict dietary laws was a matter of survival and identity.[3] Peter cringed at the thought of desecrating the dietary laws.[4] He burst out, "No way!" The vision had everything to do with a major transition the Lord wanted to take place in Peter's life. Peter's response shows his resistance to that transition.

Successful transition depends on not allowing resistance to hold you back. God was already at work in this transition from Cornelius's end. His men were journeying to find Peter and would soon be knocking on his door. Digesting the meaning of the vision went against every fiber of Peter's Jewish heritage, but he did not allow resistance to become disobedience. When the Gentile men sent by Cornelius arrived, Peter invited them into his home. He took a major step in this monumental transition by not recoiling at the idea of sharing food and lodging under the same roof with Gentiles. Through his obedience to the vision from God, he opened the door to receive Gentiles into the fellowship of the church.[5]

God repeated the vision to Peter three times to persuade him to embrace this change. He knew the transition would not be easy for Peter. How many times does God prompt you before you embrace a significant change? My goal as a Christ-follower is to be someone the Lord can lead through change with a heart that is open to transition. What about you?

Oh, by the way, repetition paid off for my husband. He passed the Jumpmaster Course as a milestone, eventually earning the status of Master Parachutist. He got a wreath around the star on his jump wings to be worn on his uniform, and I did not resist the jewel he added to the jump-wings necklace to be worn around my neck!

Respond
When have you resisted transition? Was the transition physical or spiritual? What were the reasons for your resistance?

Prayer for the journey
Lord, enlighten the eyes of my heart, that I may know the hope to which you have called me, the riches of your glorious inheritance in the saints, and the immeasurable greatness of your power toward me, according to the working of your great might. Amen. (See Ephesians 1:18–19)

Waypoint 3
Navigating with a broken compass

Read

Now while Peter was inwardly perplexed as to what the vision that he had seen might mean, behold the men who were sent by Cornelius, having made inquiry for Simon's house, stood at the gate and called out to ask whether Simon who was called Peter was lodging there. And while Peter was pondering the vision, the Spirit said to him, "Behold, three men are looking for you. Rise and go down and accompany them without hesitation, for I have sent them." (Acts 10:17–20)

Reflect

Transition can leave us disoriented, feeling like we are navigating life with a broken compass. As someone with a poor sense of direction, I need a fully operational compass. Military life and beyond presented me with numerous opportunities to travel. Even with my poor sense of direction, I have navigated trains, planes, autobahns, and subways around the world, but I sometimes get lost when attempting to navigate through a transition.

When the vision ended, Peter tried to figure out what it meant for him. God had smashed Peter's internal compass of religious rituals and the rules that had directed his life and he was perplexed. Like a trooper dropped into unfamiliar territory in the middle of night with no landmarks in sight only to discover his compass is broken, Peter was disoriented.

Scripture describes his emotion following the vision as "perplexed" as he pondered the event. A good word picture for *ponder* is that his mind was going this way and that without being able to come to any real understanding or conclusion.[6] Transition will do that to a person!

Have you ever used a compass to navigate? Compass navigation is more difficult than it sounds. You have to know exactly where you are when you start and make sure you have the compass pointed in the right direction. Then you must make sure you do not stop short of your destination, or navigate on the correct course but go too far past your destination point. A compass is a good tool, but tough to use with proficiency. There is a better way: GPS. Guided by a satellite in the sky, a GPS knows where you are, where you need to go, and best of all—how to get there. All you have to do is stay connected.

To Peter's credit, the fact that he saw this vision while he was on the rooftop, in prayer, indicates that he is in the condition to receive the message of God.[7] More important than being able to see or predict every phase of a transition is being sure our connection with God is strong. The men at Peter's door reiterated the story of the angel's visit to Cornelius, reinforcing with Peter that the vision and the men were both part of a script God was writing. Peter did not know where he was going or why, but he was willing to be led by God.[8]

Transition is the process that gets us from one place to another in the context of what could be the *new normal.* We do not just jump from a clean start to the ordered end. What happens in the middle of the process can be messy, but the mess is necessary in order to let go of prejudices, methods, and attitudes—the emotional junk that keeps us from moving forward.

As a military wife I learned to prepare for change, but it took me a while to realize I was not always prepared for transition. Checking boxes on lists for a PCS, deployment, or reintegration can indicate that things in my life changed. I cannot make a linear plan on how I will deal with the emotional struggles I experience in between change and acceptance.

I have learned, however, not to panic when my old tried-and-true compass gets smashed. I just turn on my prayer-powered GPS, focus on where I am, and take the next turn. Sister, God knows how to lead us through transition.

Respond
The danger in this stage is to "grow numb by avoidance and denial."[9] What have you done to get past avoidance and denial during transition? How has prayer prepared you for transition?

Prayer for the journey
Lord, when I feel disoriented I'm reminded of my dependence on you. Thank you for the assurance that your Spirit will help me in my weakness. When I do not know what to pray for your Spirit intercedes for me with groanings too deep for words. Amen. (See Romans 8:26.)

Waypoint 4
Something new is coming

... The next day he rose and went away with them, and some of the brothers from Joppa accompanied him. And on the following day they entered Caesarea. Cornelius was expecting them and had called together his relatives and close friends. When Peter entered, Cornelius met him and fell down at his feet and worshiped him. But Peter lifted him up, saying, "Stand up; I too am a man." And as he talked with him, he went in and found many persons gathered. And he said to them, "You yourselves know how unlawful it is for a Jew to associate with or to visit anyone of another nation, but God has shown me that I should not call any person common or unclean. So when I was sent for, I came without objection. I ask then why you sent for me." (Acts 10:23–29)

Reflect

Transition often includes new places and usually new faces. When people are a part of a transition equation, making a good first impression can pave the way for future encounters. Consider military protocol. When a military dignitary arrives, a protocol officer ensures the correct implementation of introductions, seating arrangements, and other details for a successful visit.

The meeting between Cornelius, an officer of an occupying army, and Peter, a leader of a fast-growing religious movement, could be categorized today as a Key Leader Engagement. Such an event would require a protocol officer. For Peter to enter the home of a person whom his community called a Gentile dog, and for Cornelius to acknowledge a *god* who opposed his commander-in-chief, Caesar, as a deity, was likely to be awkward on both sides. External factors surrounding this meeting likely raised the anxiety-level for this key step of transition.

If proper protocol were followed in this social climate:

1. Cornelius, a unit commander, would have traveled to seek an audience with Peter, the religious leader.
2. Peter, and the Jews with him, would have never agreed to meet in a Gentile home.
3. Cornelius would not have bowed down to Peter because it was an offense to worship anyone but God.

Who set up this meeting, anyway? Oh yeah, God! And God decided to establish his own protocol. When Peter entered the house of Cornelius he "refused both to be treated by Cornelius as if he were a god, and to treat Cornelius as if he were a dog."[10]

Peter's presence in the home of Cornelius communicates a radical adjustment in his attitude toward the Gentiles. The wall between Jews and Gentiles started to crumble as these two men responded to God's new direction.[11]

In the midst of a major transition, we may not have a good handle on the significance of the big picture. However, we can focus on those new individuals with whom we come face-to-face. When God is the protocol officer behind the scenes, every person with whom we cross paths may play an important role in God's plan, both for us and for them.

Respond

Who has played an important role in your acceptance of a change in your life? What new thing is God asking you to embrace?

Prayer for the journey

Lord, give me a willing heart to accept your direction in my life. Prepare me for any new thing you want to do in and through me. Amen.

Waypoint 5
Present for duty

Read

So Peter opened his mouth and said: "Truly I understand that God shows no partiality, but in every nation anyone who fears him and does what is right is acceptable to him. As for the word that he sent to Israel, preaching good news of peace through Jesus Christ (he is Lord of all), you yourselves know what happened throughout all Judea, beginning from Galilee after the baptism that John proclaimed: how God anointed Jesus of Nazareth with the Holy Spirit and with power. He went about doing good and healing all who were oppressed by the devil, for God was with him. (Acts 10:34–38)

Reflect

How long does it take after a PCS move before your new house feels like home? You know, that feeling like you belong and you are where you are supposed to be? Settled into your new surroundings you are ready to write the next chapter in your family saga of life in the military, and you know the read will be good!

A sign that transition has been successful is moving to the stage of acceptance. The change is complete. You are in the here and now, present for duty, and ready to get on with life.

In a few days' time, Peter transitioned from a confused person on a rooftop, trying to make sense of a disconcerting vision, to a preacher ready to break new ground in God's vineyard. No doubt he walked out his thought process over the two-day journey from Joppa to Caesarea. I wonder if one of the reasons God picked Cornelius for this transition, instead of a Gentile next door, is that he knew Peter would need a little time to process the big change that was coming. A two-day journey, probably on foot, was part of the plan.

When Peter addressed the group of Cornelius's family and close friends, he preached the first Christian sermon presented to Gentiles. Though this was a new audience for Peter, the content of the sermon was the same he had been preaching to the Jews.[12]

Peter had rapidly accepted the view that everyone was important to God. He accepted the mission from God to take the gospel to the Gentiles on their home turf. He accepted the conversion of Cornelius and those with him as legitimate. He accepted the fact that God wanted Gentiles in his church as much as he wanted Jews. He led the way in welcoming the new believers as spiritual equals through the sacrament of baptism. Peter had made a major transition in his ministry at breakneck speed.

The timeline for transition will be different for everyone. Some changes and transition come easily and quickly. Other changes drag us kicking and screaming, and the timeframe from avoidance to acceptance is longer than we want. The sooner we arrive at the transitional endpoint of acceptance, the sooner we will start looking for the good in the new phase.

Respond
What transition in your life has come quickly? What transition in your life has taken a long time? What factors made the difference in the timeline?

Prayer for the journey
Lord, help me to cooperate with your plan for my life. Thank you for the times when transition has been easy and quick. Whatever the timeline, teach me the lessons I need to learn in the process. Amen.

Waypoint 6

Esther—Seasons of transition

So when the king's order and his edict were proclaimed, and when many young women were gathered in Susa the citadel in custody of Hegai, Esther also was taken into the king's palace and put in custody of Hegai, who had charge of the women. And the young woman pleased him and won his favor. And he quickly provided her with her cosmetics and her portion of food, and with seven chosen young women from the king's palace, and advanced her and her young women to the best place in the harem. Esther had not made known her people or kindred, for Mordecai had commanded her not to make it known. And every day Mordecai walked in front of the court of the harem to learn how Esther was and what was happening to her. (Esther 2:8–11)

Reflect

You only have to look at my front door to know the season. A decorative wreath clearly communicates spring, summer, fall, or winter. Throughout the year, the seasons come and go with distinctive conditions of temperature and length of day. These God-ordained changes mark the movement of time in nature.[13]

Seasons in a person's life are not so easy to define or designate. Institutions, people, or circumstances can all initiate a new season in your life. Institutions like the military may define a season when, based on your husband's age they say, "The season of your service is over, thank you very much." A wound on a battlefield can bring an unexpected season for you and your family with a beginning and end that you cannot predict by the days on the calendar. Financial circumstances can introduce a new season, whether by an unexpected windfall of gain, or an unexpected downturn of loss. A PCS move or a new job can initiate a new season for you. New additions to your family, a child starting school, or leaving for college—are all situations that can define a season of life.

If we looked at Esther's front door we could determine the season she was experiencing, not from the color of her door hanging but from the presence and actions of her uncle Mordecai. While Esther was in a season of preparation to meet the king, Mordecai was daily at the front door of the harem court to see how she was and to make sure all was well. When *Queen* Esther was in a comfortable season of feasting, Mordecai's place at the front door allowed him to overhear a plot against the king that he passed on to Esther allowing her to gain favor from the ruler. Later, Mordecai's presence at the front door, while dressed in sackcloth, signaled the coming of an unwelcomed and alarming season of risk and potential death for Esther and the Jews.

Just as we cannot control the seasons of our life, Esther was not in control of the circumstances that marked her seasons. Take some time to read all nine chapters of the book of Esther—it is quite a story! This young Jewish woman ended up in the harem of the King of Persia. Through a type of ancient beauty pageant, the king chose her to be his new queen without knowing her nationality. Could God use a Jewish girl in a pagan palace? Esther's seasons in the palace were not by chance, and her purpose there would become clear.[14]

Just as spring seems to pass quickly and winter seems to drag on forever, some seasons of life may feel rushed while other seasons wear out their welcome. We cannot control when they start and when they end, but we can rest assured that God can bring purpose to each season. A fulfilled life results when we learn how to celebrate the good that God can bring in every season of life.

Reflect

Seasons of life are not necessarily a result of age, but of circumstance. How would you describe your current season? Depending on the circumstances, entering a new season can be intimidating. Rather than dread a future season, determine to live with purpose in every season. Consider these questions when you navigate a new season:

- What are the lessons to be learned in this season?
- What are the blessings for which I should be grateful in this season?
- What opportunities can I find to serve others in this season?
- What does God want me to leave behind in this season?

Prayer for the journey

Lord, help me to discern your purpose for the season of life in which I find myself. Like the psalmist, "I cry out to God Most High, to God who fulfills his purpose for me" (Psalm 57:2). Amen.

Waypoint 7

I've got rhythm

If it please the king, let it be decreed that they be destroyed, and I will pay 10,000 talents of silver into the hands of those who have charge of the king's business, that they may put it into the king's treasuries." So the king took his signet ring from his hand and gave it to Haman the Agagite, the son of Hammedatha, the enemy of the Jews. And the king said to Haman, "The money is given to you, the people also, to do with them as it seems good to you." (Esther 3:9–11)

Reflect

"What is your goal for this year?" asked my friend. I chuckle now over my intensely serious response, "Balance. I want to have balance in my life." I'm not sure what my younger thirty-something mind and heart considered balance, but my older (and a bit wiser) self realizes that balance is an unattainable goal.

Margaret Feinberg offers a spot-on reason for balance as an unrealistic objective: "Sometimes life picks up speed without warning or slows down unexpectedly. Sometimes we're pulled in many directions all at once. Sometimes we find ourselves pushed by our schedules, commitments, and unexpected needs in life. And any sense of balance is lost."[15]

Military wives can certainly identify with the push of schedules, commitments, and life's unexpected needs. Trying to keep all of these in perfect balance would be exhausting! No sooner would you get the plates spinning in synchronization, than something will come along to upset the momentum, and an inevitable crash happens. I suggest we replace the quest for balance with the acceptance of rhythm. Each season brings a new rhythm in which to keep time.

When the king selected Esther to be his queen, the trajectory of her life took a drastic turn. Her rhythm could have been one of others catering to her every need. I imagine royal servants on her right and left, perfectly poised to respond to any whim. She only needed to sit tight and enjoy her new life.

Esther's life in the palace of the king caused her to enter into a rhythm she did not create. The wicked palace official Haman developed a plan to annihilate the Jews. He convinced the king that since the Jewish people did not follow the customs or appreciate the laws of the Persian king, they were of no use. The king's signing and sealing of the decree with his signet ring set the destructive event in motion. Esther was forced into a season with a rhythm beating toward a crescendo of destruction already made law. Would she sit on the sideline and watch or would she play her part in the rhythm already in progress?

What we cannot see in this story is the obvious presence of God. In fact, the book of Esther does not mention God. Yet, God set the divine metronome beating out the rhythm for all the events in the book. What looked like coincidence in the life of Esther was God working to save a people who, generations later, would birth the Savior of the world.

Respond
How do you try to find balance in your life? What difference does it make to find the correct rhythm during your seasons of life as opposed to finding balance?

Prayer for the journey
Lord, I can exhaust myself trying to balance all my schedules, relationships, and responsibilities. Help me let you set the pace for my life for this season, for this day, and always. Amen.

Waypoint 8
Time travel

"All the king's servants and the people of the king's provinces know that if any man or woman goes to the king inside the inner court without being called, there is but one law—to be put to death, except the one to whom the king holds out the golden scepter so that he may live. But as for me, I have not been called to come in to the king these thirty days." And they told Mordecai what Esther had said. Then Mordecai told them to reply to Esther, "Do not think to yourself that in the king's palace you will escape any more than all the other Jews. For if you keep silent at this time, relief and deliverance will rise for the Jews from another place, but you and your father's house will perish. And who knows whether you have not come to the kingdom for such a time as this?"

Then Esther told them to reply to Mordecai, "Go, gather all the Jews to be found in Susa, and hold a fast on my behalf, and do not eat or drink for three days, night or day. I and my young women will also fast as you do. Then I will go to the king, though it is against the law, and if I perish, I perish." (Esther 4:11–16)

Reflect

Do you notice how we often anticipate one calendar season only to tire of it quickly and pine for the next? I looked at the calendar this morning and saw in black and white that a new season is fast approaching. Crisp, cool days of autumn will soon replace the sticky hot days of summer. Why does it seem like summer is always on speed dial? Unlike retail stores that already display Christmas decorations, I want to draw out the days of autumn. (Yes, I'm one of those people who refuse to put up anything red or green until after Thanksgiving.) Then winter will arrive and feel to me like it will never end. Within its long drawn out days I will long for spring to take a short cut. Discontent finds its way into every calendar season.

I frequently find the same discontent when I reflect upon seasons of life. In such moments, I recognize my capacity to engage in *time travel*. Please don't think I'm speaking of a mystical quantum-mechanics experience. No, I'm referring to my tendency to look back to the last life season, or ahead to the next season, rather than embracing fully the season of today. I can live in such hurried anticipation of new orders, a deployment ending, the age of my kids, or a negative work situation that I miss the purpose of *now*. My discontent and worry propel me forward in anticipation, or backward in longing.

Esther faced a defining moment which no doubt brought anxiety and a desire to travel through time to a place where responsibility was not as heavy. Mordecai discovered Haman's plan to annihilate the Jews and sent word to Esther asking her to appeal to the king on behalf of the Jews. Esther replied that the king would interpret such an act as treason. Besides, he did not even know she was a Jew.

Mordecai asked Esther to reveal her identity at the riskiest time. Up to now, Esther went along with the flow and it served her well. Her circumstances had controlled her season as she followed the path of least resistance.[16] Suddenly she faced the decision to take responsibility for not only herself, but also her nation and rise to the occasion.[17] She did not choose this moment—the moment chose her. Esther's first choice may have been time travel, but she did not have that option, and neither do we. She chose option two: rise to the occasion.

Sister, we cannot afford to pine for the past or long for the future. God calls us to face each day with the determination to live out his purpose for that day. Anxiety and worry rob us of living in the present and produce discontent. They are the fuel of *time travel.* The Scriptures exhort us to steward the season in which we find ourselves. Just as Esther lived out her purpose in a king's palace, God has a purpose for you to live out today. Don't allow discontent and anxiety to thwart God's purpose *for such a time as this.*

Respond
What does Jesus have to say about anxiety and worry in Matthew 6:19–25? What part have worry and anxiety played in robbing you of living in the present?

Prayer for the journey
Lord, forgive me when I look with longing to the way things were in the past or the way I want them to be in the future. Teach me how to live in the present with ever increasing joy and gratitude. Amen.

Waypoint 9
Return to your roots

Read

So the king and Haman went in to feast with Queen Esther. And on the second day, as they were drinking wine after the feast, the king again said to Esther, "What is your wish, Queen Esther? It shall be granted you. And what is your request? Even to the half of my kingdom, it shall be fulfilled. Then Queen Esther answered, "If I have found favor in your sight, O king, and if it please the king, let my life be granted me for my wish, and my people for my request. For we have been sold, I and my people, to be destroyed, to be killed, and to be annihilated. If we had been sold merely as slaves, men and women, I would have been silent, for our affliction is not to be compared with the loss to the king." (Esther 7:1–5)

Reflect

Did you notice the bombshell Esther dropped in her speech to the king? Up to this time, her ethnicity was a secret. Only her uncle Mordecai knew she was a Jew. Five years had passed since Esther became queen.[18] Do you think she thought she would ever return to her Jewish roots? We cannot know the answer, but we know that by identifying herself with the Jewish people Esther took a huge risk that could have resulted in her death.

I never had a desire to reconnect with my Tennessee roots. To revise an outdated phrase—I had been there, done that, and I did not want a new tee-shirt. Upon military retirement, guess where a job opened for my husband that perfectly fit his skill set and experience? Yep, my hometown in Tennessee!

Few of us face such a monumental risk as Esther when we reconnect with our roots. My life or the continuance of my family line was not at stake when I returned to Tennessee. Yet returning to my roots brought unexpected challenges. In some ways, it felt like death to a way of life.

I do not want to trivialize this crisis point in Esther's story by comparing it to my own struggle of returning to my roots. But there are some principles to apply. Returning to my roots was associated with a risk of not being able to fulfill my aspirations and dreams. I felt like I was going backward instead of forward. More importantly, I was uncertain my return to Tennessee was in God's timetable at the start of a new season of life.

At a minimum, Esther's identification with her Jewish roots could have meant a complete lifestyle change.. The king could easily have escorted her out the gates of the palace. At a maximum, Esther's announcement could have labeled her for destruction along with the Jewish people.

Whether relocating to your hometown or a new city, transitioning out of the known lifestyle of the military into an uncertain way of life has inherent risks. Though it is important to evaluate the risks involved with a major change, it is more important to discern what the will of God is for you. Esther was willing to accept the risks associated with her Jewish roots. She believed her place in the palace, at that time, was for a purpose greater than herself.

Respond

When has thinking "I thought things would be different" fueled discontent in your life? How did you navigate that season of life?

Prayer for the journey

Lord, thank you for the gift of life. Thank you for the circumstances that have brought me to this place. Help me trust that I am exactly where I am meant to be. Amen.

Waypoint 10
A brave choice remembered

Read

Now the rest of the Jews who were in the king's provinces also gathered to defend their lives, and got relief from their enemies and killed 75,000 of those who hated them, but they laid no hands on the plunder. This was on the thirteenth day of the month of Adar, and on the fourteenth day they rested and made that a day of feasting and gladness. But the Jews who were in Susa gathered on the thirteenth day and on the fourteenth, and rested on the fifteenth day, making that a day of feasting and gladness. Therefore the Jews of the villages, who live in the rural towns, hold the fourteenth day of the month of Adar as a day for gladness and feasting, as a holiday, and as a day on which they send gifts of food to one another. (Esther 9:16–19)

Reflect

"Brenda, you are part of our institutional history," were the unforgettable words spoken to me about my involvement in a military organization. At forty years old, I was just told I was historical. Now, I could have interpreted the words to mean I was a relic whose time had passed, but I choose to accept the affirmation for my earlier decision to participate wholeheartedly in an organization I valued. I was part of a leadership team whose contributions over the years had been institutionalized to the extent that they would continue to make a positive difference for those who would follow.

Esther was still a young woman when she made the choice to put her life at risk, identify with her people, and confront her enemy. Her action resulted in the Jewish people celebrating a victory over potential destruction, which they then institution-alized.[19] Jews still commemorate Esther's choice in the festival of Purim. Esther 9:27–29 makes the celebration of this event a holy obligation, not just an optional observance, from that time forward. Jews worldwide maintain their obligation to celebrate Purim as days when God gave them relief from their enemies, turned their sorrow into gladness, and their mourning into joy.[20]

What would have happened if Esther's choice had been different? Her circumstances forced a choice between saving her people and protecting herself. God might have raised up someone else to bring deliverance and we would not remember her. But she made a hard and wise choice in an uncertain season.

Each season of life brings opportunities to make contributions that benefit others. I must weigh my decisions today in light of the consequences of tomorrow, both for others and for myself. Only God knows if the seasons to follow will validate my choices of today.

We celebrate Esther's choice to identify with God's people. The most important choice we can make is to identify ourselves with God's people by accepting Jesus as our Savior. That choice will make a difference in every season of life. Now, that is something to celebrate!

Respond

How have you seen choices someone made as a young woman affect them in a negative or positive way in later years? What can you learn from such examples? What has God done for you in this season of your life that you can celebrate?

Prayer for the journey

Lord, help me make wise choices today that will have a positive impact on the future. Make me brave in every season of life. Amen.

Waypoint 11
Naomi and Ruth—Unwelcomed transitions

In the days when the judges ruled there was a famine in the land, and a man of Bethlehem in Judah went to sojourn in the country of Moab, he and his wife and his two sons. The name of the man was Elimelech and the name of his wife Naomi, and the names of his two sons were Mahlon and Chilion. They were Ephrathites from Bethlehem in Judah. They went into the country of Moab and remained there. But Elimelech, the husband of Naomi, died, and she was left with her two sons. These took Moabite wives; the name of the one was Orpah and the name of the other Ruth. They lived there about ten years, and both Mahlon and Chilion died, so that the woman was left without her two sons and her husband. (Ruth 1:1–5)

Reflect

Do you think Naomi ever said, "When I grow up, I want a famine to come and force my family to move to a foreign country where my husband and two sons will die, leaving me two foreign daughters-in-law as my only family?" Of course not! Scripture never suggests Naomi deserved or desired the tragic events behind her unexpected transition. Living in an imperfect world exposes us to tragedy and disappointment and forces us to adapt. Naomi was at the intersection of tragedy and transition.

Military culture can also precipitate hard, unwanted transitions that test a wife's resilience. The basic mechanics of how the military functions come with built-in consequences of hardship for some. The military's rank structure produces promotion parties for those selected to advance in rank and quiet grieving for those who are not. The military's mission to protect the nation produces cheering citizens along a parade route for those who survive combat and somber processions at a national cemetery for those who do not. Military wives do not get to choose where they will be standing with their husband.

Naomi has something to say to military wives who face unwanted and unexpected transitions. She did not coast through her tragedies as an unscathed observer. She was devastated. Later in Ruth 1:20, Naomi says, "Do not call me Naomi [Sweet one]; call me Mara [Bitter one],[21] for the Almighty has dealt very bitterly with me." In her worldview, God was responsible for what had happened in her life.[22] When you consider Naomi's dire situation, her bitter outlook on life and her questioning of God's role in it all are understandable.

But don't write her off too soon, because even at her lowest point, she was a survivor—in fact, she thrived! When she lost everything in Moab, she took the next step to journey home to Bethlehem. Through a chain of unexpected good events, God raised Naomi from her lowest point of despair to an elevated position in a distinguished family lineage in Israel. He took her bitter heart and sweetened it with his divine blessings.

Sister, we can find hope as we observe Naomi's life journey. In the darkest hours, the Lord can shine a light to help us find our way through the most difficult transitions.

Respond

When have you experienced an unexpected and unwanted transition? How did you get through that difficult time?

Prayer for the journey

Lord, help me trust you even in times when I do not understand what is happening. Protect my heart from bitterness so the work of your Spirit in my life will flourish. Amen.

Waypoint 12
Ruth and the elephant in the room

Read

And [Naomi] said, "See, your sister-in-law has gone back to her people and to her gods; return after your sister-in-law." But Ruth said, "Do not urge me to leave you or to return from following you. For where you go I will go, and where you lodge I will lodge. Your people shall be my people, and your God my God. Where you die I will die, and there will I be buried. May the Lord do so to me and more also if anything but death parts me from you." And when Naomi saw that she was determined to go with her, she said no more. (Ruth 1:15–18)

Reflect

The elephant in the room (or on Facebook) after the publication of a military promotion list is who made the list and who did not. The easiest phone call to make is to congratulate a friend on their husband's selection for promotion. The hardest, and one we often put off, is to the friend whose husband did not read his name on the list. Why do we tend to avoid interaction with those who have received potentially devastating news? Non-selection for a promotion, a frightening diagnosis, a soured relationship—whatever the difficulty, we can feel awkward and not know what to say. We do not want to say something to make the situation worse, so too often we do not say anything.

Naomi decided that no one needed to be around her in her disappointment. She told her daughters-in-law to leave. She would face misery alone. This would be her solitary misfortune.[23]

Then there was Ruth. Determined could have been her middle name. Naomi argued logically and emphatically why

Ruth should leave. Staying meant subjecting herself to Naomi's doom and despair.[24] But Ruth's affirming words halted further discussion. That girl was not leaving Naomi, and her choice changed the trajectory of both their lives. Ruth did not have all the right answers or have the ability to make things okay again. But unexpected tragedy brought an unexpected response from her. Something in her made her want to be by Naomi's side, regardless of the future. In a time of grief and confusion, Ruth pledged her companionship. She promised to continue the journey with Naomi, accept Naomi's people, worship Naomi's God, and end her days in the same place as Naomi.

From the perspective of the person dealing with unexpected transition like Naomi, even though we may want to deal with sorrow alone, we need not push others away. Appreciate the person who does not try to fix what is wrong, but who is willing to offer presence and support. From the perspective of the person who wants to help, like Ruth, affirm your commitment and find a way to reach out without invading privacy. In the hardest times of my life, I do not remember words said, but I remember people who were with me.

Ruth became the link to the restoration of Naomi's life. You never know when you may be the key link for another by standing with them during a challenging season.

Respond

How has the presence of another person helped you during a difficult or traumatic event? How tough is it for you to accept help during such times?

Prayer for the journey

Lord, help me be a loyal and supportive presence when friends and family go through difficult transitions. Help me to be willing to accept help during my own times of struggle. Thank you that you are an ever-present help in time of need. Amen.

Waypoint 13
When I cannot see you

Now Naomi had a relative of her husband's, a worthy man of the clan of Elimelech, whose name was Boaz. And Ruth the Moabite said to Naomi, "Let me go to the field and glean among the ears of grain after him in whose sight I shall find favor." And she said to her, "Go, my daughter." So she set out and went and gleaned in the field after the reapers and she happened to come to the part of the field belonging to Boaz who was of the clan of Elimelech. (Ruth 2:1–3)

Reflect

Where is God in this situation? Why is this happening to me? These common questions push their way through the lips of those experiencing tough situations. Whether attributed to the military or a personal crisis common to anyone, such questions are an honest expression of despair and indicate that life from this point will be different.

Life for Naomi and Ruth certainly took a different turn. Their unwanted status as widows flipped Naomi and Ruth's place in society upside down. In a patriarchal culture, they lost their identity and security.[25] A wife who hears her husband say he wants a divorce, or a woman who loses her child can feel this same sense of loss. Life as we know it can change in a moment. We look around and ask, "God, where are you? Why is this happening to me?"

Sister, can I tell you God is there, even when you do not see him? Naomi and Ruth discovered God's presence when they were trying to find a way to survive. Ruth did what she had to do to put bread on the table. Gleaning in the field was her culture's method of food stamp distribution. Hebrew law allowed the poor to gather the leftover grain after the harvest. God established the principle to provide for the poor (Deuteronomy 24:19–21). No doubt Ruth was among other poor folks in the community looking for the bits of grain left behind.

Scripture uses an interesting phrase to describe the scene. Ruth *"happened* to come upon the field" of a distant wealthy relative (Ruth 2:3). Before we jump to the end of the story, we need to pause and note that the concept of fate, luck, or chance cannot be read into this verse; that is not the Old Testament view of God's sovereignty.[26] The writer of Ruth emphasized that the human initiative of Ruth or Boaz did not orchestrate this event. Rather, the hand of God was working behind the scenes.[27]

Not only do we see the hand of God directing Ruth to the right field, but God also put compassion and concern into the heart of Boaz for the young Moabite woman who had made it her responsibility to care for her mother-in-law. When Naomi learned where Ruth had been and heard the favor that she received from Boaz, it gave her a spark of hope to think that God's invisible hand was working on their behalf.

Respond
How does Matthew 28:20b answer the question, "Where is God in this situation?" How do James 1:2–4 and 1 Corinthians 13:9–10, 12 give you hope when you find yourself asking the question, "Why is this happening to me?"

Prayer for the journey
Lord, remind me you are always at work even when I do not recognize your actions. Give me a determined mind and heart to trust you and rest in the promise of your care. Amen.

Waypoint 14
One step at a time

Then Naomi her mother-in-law said to her, "My daughter, should I not seek rest for you, that it may be well with you? Is not Boaz our relative, with whose young women you were? See, he is winnowing barley tonight at the threshing floor. Wash therefore and anoint yourself, and put on your cloak and go down to the threshing floor, but do not make yourself known to the man until he has finished eating and drinking. But when he lies down, observe the place where he lies. Then go and uncover his feet and lie down, and he will tell you what to do." And she replied, "All that you say I will do." (Ruth 3:1–5)

Reflect

Ruth took the step she knew to take—a step of survival to glean in the field among the poor. Naomi saw the next step forward when she realized that, according to their culture, Boaz would be an acceptable relative to take Ruth as a wife. She instructed Ruth on the appropriate method to propose marriage to Boaz.[28] Things looked more hopeful than they had in a long time!

Before we sing, "Here Comes the Bride," realize that this was not the final step bringing Ruth and Boaz to the altar. Another man had first rights to marry Ruth and acquire her father-in-law's land. Isn't that the way life often goes? We take one step, then another, but there is no guarantee things will work out for good. Each step is a step of faith. We rarely complete major transitions with one giant step. Nor must we take unlimited baby steps to get where we need to be. Hope arrives when we recognize the Lord can order our steps as we look to him for help.

The words of Taya Kyle, wife of murdered Navy SEAL Chris Kyle, make this principle personal. This is from a letter she wrote for the "Note to Self" series on CBS *This Morning*:

Dear Taya, There's so much I could tell you that you're going to experience—joy beyond your wildest dreams, and a grief so terrible you'll be sure it will break you. I wish I could keep you from the pain, but life isn't like that.

When you're in your early twenties, you will meet a man who will change your life. His name is Chris Kyle … The two of you will fall madly in love and decide to spend the rest of your lives together.

Chris is a Navy SEAL. He believes in God, Country, and Family, just like you do. He'll serve four tours in Iraq. Then, finally, he'll come home. Things will seem … perfect. Until one day, one horrible, terrible, very long day, the very worst will happen when you least expect it.

It's not going to be easy. In the end you'll reach deep inside yourself to find the strength to carry through. Try and remember these things as you go on your journey: You like to be independent but you will need to learn to ask for help. It doesn't make you weak.

Sometimes you will think you can't take it another day. But if you hang in there, one step at a time, you will be able to accomplish more than you ever imagine.[29]

Respond

Ruth and Naomi had no idea how their story would end, yet they kept taking steps forward. What keeps you moving forward when it would be easier to quit? What does it mean to you to take steps of faith?

Prayer for the journey

Lord, sometimes taking the next step feels risky. You alone know what it brings. Let my steps today be ordered by you. Amen.

Waypoint 15
A day redefined

Read

So Boaz took Ruth, and she became his wife. And he went in to her, and the LORD gave her conception, and she bore a son. Then the women said to Naomi, "Blessed be the LORD, who has not left you this day without a redeemer, and may his name be renowned in Israel! He shall be to you a restorer of life and a nourisher of your old age, for your daughter-in-law who loves you, who is more to you than seven sons, has given birth to him." Then Naomi took the child and laid him on her lap and became his nurse. And the women of the neighborhood gave him a name, saying, "A son has been born to Naomi." They named him Obed. He was the father of Jesse, the father of David. (Ruth 4:13–17)

Reflect

I looked with dread at the day circled on the calendar. The anniversary of my father's death was imminent. Other than my husband, my dad was my greatest cheerleader and source of emotional support. Our family misses his kindness, wisdom, and sacrificial love. But something happened this year to change the way I view this anniversary. A sweet little granddaughter was born! A day that sorrow had overshadowed is now a day filled with joy. I will not forget my father's death, but the day has been redefined from one of sorrow to one of joy.

Naomi would have taken it as a cruel joke if someone had told her, after she lost her husband and sons in a foreign land, "Take heart! One day you will hold in your arms a grandson who will be the grandfather of Israel's greatest king!" Yet that is exactly what happened!

Ruth 4 is the story of Boaz making Ruth his wife, a story of redemption that redefined the sorrow not only of Ruth, but of Naomi. A baby was born and God gave Naomi a new reason to live—a blessing she could hold in her arms.[30] But Naomi's redemption went far beyond the joy of holding Obed. Her blessing became a testimony to her neighbors.

The book ends with a genealogy of Obed's son and grandson, Jesse and David (Ruth 4:18–22). This inclusion can seem an afterthought, but you don't want to miss the meaning. It communicates God's providence and care beyond the life of one woman. Obed's birth takes on new significance when you trace his lineage to David, who played a significant role in the redemption of an entire nation. Then trace David's lineage to the birth of Jesus in the New Testament book of Matthew. Do you see it? Nestled in God's redemption for Naomi was the seed of his plan of redemption for the world through Jesus Christ.[31]

My sister, it is always easier to identify the hand of God looking backward rather than forward into the unknown. When going through a season of transition, do not attempt to tie God's hands or fail to look at what he is doing. Have faith in all that God is going to do. He can more than salvage a situation—God can redeem it and make it new!

Respond

How does the story of Ruth and Naomi give you hope and courage for times of difficult transition? How does God's kindness demonstrated in this book encourage you?

Prayer for the journey

Lord, you are a God who can exchange tragedy for hope. "Because your loving kindness is better than life, my lips will praise you" (Psalm 63:3 NASB). Amen.

Waypoint 16

Caleb: A man with no regrets

Read

Then the people of Judah came to Joshua at Gilgal. And Caleb the son of Jephunneh the Kenizzite said to him, "You know what the LORD said to Moses the man of God in Kadesh-barnea concerning you and me. I was forty years old when Moses the servant of the LORD sent me from Kadesh-barnea to spy out the land, and I brought him word again as it was in my heart. But my brothers who went up with me made the heart of the people melt; yet I wholly followed the LORD my God. And Moses swore on that day, saying, 'Surely the land on which your foot has trodden shall be an inheritance for you and your children forever, because you have wholly followed the LORD my God.' And now, behold, the LORD has kept me alive, just as he said, these forty-five years since the time that the LORD spoke this word to Moses, while Israel walked in the wilderness. And now, behold, I am this day eighty-five years old." (Joshua 14:6–10)

Reflect

He did not have a photo showing how long his hair was before he joined the military. He did not use a PowerPoint slideshow to trace his career from the proud smile on his face from initial training graduation, through various promotions with significant friends, to his last official photo displaying his awards and decorations. But in his own way Caleb reflected on his years of service leading to the occasion in today's passage where he was ready to transition to a new era in his life.

Caleb recounted his faithful service to Joshua, the leader who succeeded Moses. Of those present, Joshua best knew Caleb and his life. Out of twelve men sent out by Moses to spy out the land promised by God, these two were the only ones left—the ones who had declared that, with God's help, the Israelites could defeat the armies they would face. The other ten spies, with the majority of Israelites of military service age, had outvoted Caleb and Joshua. Now all those who chose not to follow the Lord's plan had died in the wanderings in the wilderness. Caleb's summary was not only to remind Joshua, but all the Israelites, that God is faithful to those who determine to serve him.[32]

What did Caleb highlight at this point of transition? His faithfulness to follow the Lord, even when his peers did not. He spoke of God's promise to bless him and his family with an inheritance of land. And he reminded everyone that he had given forty-five years of faithful service with no regrets.

Military retirement is a notable accomplishment and a significant transition point for both the service member and their family. A retirement ceremony allows for a pause in mission to provide opportunity for a person to recount and reflect on the most important aspects of a career. Along with accolades, awards, and accomplishments, the person who acknowledges the hand of God and help from the Lord is the one who is best prepared for the next step off the parade field into the civilian community.

Respond

If you have attended a military retirement ceremony, what were the elements that made it meaningful? How important is it to reflect on the past during a significant transition?

Prayer for the journey

Lord, remind me of the importance of my faithfulness today, so that at the end of my journey, I may receive your blessing, "Well done, good and faithful servant" (Matthew 25:23a). Amen.

Waypoint 17

As strong as ever

"And now, behold, I am this day eighty-five years old. I am still as strong today as I was in the day that Moses sent me; my strength now is as my strength was then, for war and for going and coming." (Joshua 14:10b–11)

Reflect

If you see your husband standing bare-chested and flexing his muscles in front of a mirror on his retirement day, just humor him. Though the military demands a high standard of physical fitness, the physique on display in the mirror is probably not the one with which he started his military career. Caleb, on the other hand, professed to being as strong at age eighty-five as he was at age forty. People did live longer in biblical times, but you might have to check with Mrs. Caleb, who saw him behind closed doors, to know if he was talking about pure physical strength.

Regardless of your perspective, I have heard it said that retirement is not for weaklings. Caleb approached this major life transition—from being a traveler in the wilderness to becoming a settler in the promised land of Canaan—from a position of strength. He could still fight like a warrior and carry out the daily duties of life.[33]

Good health gives you more options when transitioning to retirement, but strength of character will help you step into retirement on the right foot. Successful military service demands fortitude, yet the same strong determination to make a significant contribution with your life is a key to fulfillment after your ID card changes categories.

The strength between your ears and the courage inside your chest is more important in a major transition than the size of your biceps and the firmness of your abdominal muscles. Acknowledging the Lord as your source of strength will give you boldness like Caleb to see your transition to retirement as the next step in God's plan for your life.

Respond
Why is it important to be a wise steward of physical health as you think about retirement? What are your goals for your physical health into retirement years?

Prayer for the journey
Lord, help me care for my body, so I may be strong enough to live out your purpose for my life, as long as I dwell on this earth. Amen.

Waypoint 18

A rocking chair or giants?

Read

"So now give me this hill country of which the LORD spoke on that day, for you heard on that day how the Anakim were there, with great fortified cities. It may be that the LORD will be with me, and I shall drive them out just as the LORD said." (Joshua 14:12)

Reflect

What do you see when you transition to retirement? A rocking chair on the back porch or a huge challenge filled with giant obstacles? If anyone had the right to ask for a rocking chair, it was Caleb. If the parents of those around Caleb now had listened to him when they left Egypt, they all could have enjoyed the good life in Canaan. As a reward for trying to do what was right, Caleb had to travel through the desert for forty years while he watched his peers depart the earth. Yes, if anyone could have said, "I deserve to take it easy now," it was Caleb.[34]

But Caleb did not ask for a rocking chair. He asked for the hill country where Hebron was located. Before he could enjoy his mountain retreat, Caleb would have to defeat the Anakim— also known as GIANTS—who lived in fortified cities. It would be difficult enough to tackle the task of conquering a fortified city, located on high ground, using swords and spears. Add giants to the mix and you intensify the challenge! Caleb entered this life transition by setting the bar of success exceptionally high.

Our communities need retiring military families to set high bars for success in civilian life. A friend of mine recently retired from the military to accept a position as a middle school teacher.

Talk about a challenge! Another person I know enrolled in a graduate degree program to better equip herself to help others. Second-career military retirees are found everywhere in our society from local pulpits to state legislatures. Any profession that needs a person to step up and lead the way is ideal for someone who has made a career of stepping up as military families have done.

Military retirement is not just a retirement from the military; it can also be a transition to the next phase of life. The day may come when getting all the way to the back porch to sit in a rocking chair is about all you are capable of doing. Until then, set high goals for the next phase of your life. Do not let giant obstacles and fortified barriers discourage you from reaching for the heights. The military encourages setting goals and finding ways to reach those goals. Military retirement means leaving the uniform behind while taking the *can-do* spirit with you.

Respond

How has military life helped you set and reach goals? What goals do you have for life after military retirement?

Prayer for the journey

Lord, as I look to the future, help me make goals that align with your will and purpose for my life. Amen.

Waypoint 19
Full sails

Read

Then Joshua blessed him, and he gave Hebron to Caleb the son of Jephunneh for an inheritance. Therefore Hebron became the inheritance of Caleb the son of Jephunneh the Kenizzite to this day, because he wholly followed the LORD, the God of Israel. (Joshua 14:13–14)

But my servant Caleb, because he has a different spirit and has followed me fully, I will bring into the land into which he went, and his descendants shall possess it. (Numbers 14:24)

Reflect

Caleb had a stellar reputation with God—and God's people. God took special notice of Caleb early on when he pronounced his judgment on the Israelites who chose not to move immediately from Egypt to Canaan because they feared the inhabitants. God declared that none of the men who came out of Egypt would set foot in the Promised Land, with the exception of Caleb and Joshua. Singling out Caleb, God said, "He has a different spirit and has followed me fully." Forty-five years later, God attributed Caleb's success in the transition to his inheritance in Hebron directly to Caleb's choice to *wholly* follow the Lord.

Scripture uses an interesting Hebrew word to describe how Caleb followed the Lord. Both of today's Scripture selections use the same root word. In Joshua 14:14 it is translated as *wholly* and in Numbers 14:24 it is translated as *fully*. The word describes something that has reached full capacity. In his commentary on

Joshua, Kenneth Gangel explains that the word is a nautical term to describe a ship with all its sails full of wind pushing straight toward a location, no matter what.[35]

When my husband and I first moved into military quarters, we were setting out in uncharted waters. We believed that this major life transition was God's will for us. I did my best to *fully* embrace the role of military wife. After nearly thirty years, traversing the globe as a military family had become the comfortable norm. Charting a new course out of the military and into retirement seems like sailing into unfamiliar waters once again. However, I am determined to *fully* embrace this new phase of God's plan. Following God with full sails is the key to success in times of transition.

God said that Caleb had a spirit different from his peers. Having a passion to fully follow the Lord was the exception in Caleb's day, and possibly in our day. Jesus said the greatest commandment is to "Love the Lord your God with all your heart and with all your soul and with all your mind" (Matthew 22:37). Living out our love for God by following where he leads can help us approach a major transition with a fully committed attitude. Who knows? We may even get a reputation like Caleb's.

Respond

What does wholly following the Lord look like to you? How does Caleb's example challenge you as you look toward retirement?

Prayer for the journey

Lord, as the psalmist declares: "Give me understanding, that I may keep your law and observe it with my whole heart" (Psalm 119:34). Amen.

Waypoint 20
Set up for success

And Caleb said, "He who attacks Kiriath-sepher and captures it, I will give him Achsah my daughter for a wife." And Othniel the son of Kenaz, Caleb's younger brother, captured it. And he gave him Achsah his daughter for a wife." (Judges 1:12–13)

My friend Victoria repeats (and practices) the statement: "Set them up for success." The "them" to whom she refers are young military wives. Upon military retirement, Victoria's husband became a civilian contractor at the local military installation. As a retired military spouse, Victoria remains active in the military community, but her role has shifted from prominent leader to prominent mentor. She uses the knowledge and experience she gained during her husband's years of military service to mentor young military wives. She has not tried to hold on to assumed power because of her longevity. Instead, she teaches classes, facilitates leadership retreats, and spends many one-on-one hours encouraging young women to be leaders in their homes and communities. She sets them up for success!

Caleb was a leader who set others up for success. Consider his actions with Othniel in Judges 1:12–13. He did not hang on to his position nor look at the next generation as a threat to his power. He fought alongside the younger men to rid the land of giants, but he knew it was time for a transition of leadership. He communicated his confidence in the next generation by presenting a challenge to them that would require risk, but would produce great reward. In offering his daughter's hand in marriage, he found someone who would care for his daughter when he was gone. Caleb may not have known who would accept the challenge, but he offered his full support to the one who did. We find in Judges 3:9 that the Lord later raised up Othniel as a deliverer and leader of Israel. Scripture suggests Caleb played a role in educating and preparing the next generation to enter the promised land.[36]

As military retirees, whether you decide to settle close to a military installation and stay involved in that community, or you completely "civilianize" your life, you have much to offer others. Your life as a military spouse has afforded rich and varied experiences that can bring a perspective from which others can benefit. Formal mentoring programs can be helpful, but the best mentoring takes place when you make yourself available to listen and offer support. You may not feel like an expert at military life—or life in general—but you can be a positive influence and a champion for young women in the throes of a new job, a new child, a new home, a new marriage, or a new relationship with Jesus.

Respond

In what ways do you set others up for success? How has someone set you up for success? What does Proverbs 27:17, Psalm 145:4, and Psalm 71:18 say about setting others up for success?

Prayer for the journey

Lord, give me a willing heart that eagerly sets up others for success. Prepare me to be a champion for the next generation. Amen.

Waypoint 21
The road to Emmaus—a heart transition

Read

That very day two of them were going to a village named Emmaus, about seven miles from Jerusalem, and they were talking with each other about all these things that had happened. While they were talking and discussing together, Jesus himself drew near and went with them. But their eyes were kept from recognizing him. And he said to them, "What is this conversation that you are holding with each other as you walk?" And they stood still, looking sad. (Luke 24:13–17)

Reflect

My husband recounts an embarrassing experience as a brand-new military chaplain. He visited a training site to talk with recruits going through initial entry training. As he came to the wooded area the only men present were the sergeants-in-charge. He asked one, "Where are the troops?" The sergeant motioned towards the trees and replied, "Right there." My husband looked around and saw no one. Puzzled, he asked again. At the order of, "On your feet," 150 well-camouflaged troops rose from the underbrush, some only steps away from my husband. The troops were right in front of him, but he could not see them.

The disciples on the Emmaus road experienced a similar event with Jesus. They were walking home from Jerusalem, sad and confused, trying to make sense of the past few days. They had watched the one whom they thought was going to be the redeemer of Israel executed on a cross and sealed in a tomb. Now three days later, some of the women said they had seen him, and the body of Jesus was gone. What was going on?

Jesus caught up with the two as they walked and asked them what they were discussing. They had probably seen him many times, but the pair did not recognize Jesus. Scripture says "their eyes were kept from recognizing him." If I had been Jesus on this occasion, I would have grabbed the two around the neck and said, "Hey guys, cheer up. It's me!" Instead, he joined their journey and added words of hope to their conversation.

Something mystically beautiful strikes me when I think of Jesus walking with them in their darkest hour. As questions filled their minds, as sorrow filled their hearts, as their purposes and plans had just died on a cross, Jesus walked with them. Jesus modeled for us what to do when someone is hurting and looking for answers and meaning during a difficult time in their life.

Jesus joined them where they were physically and began to take them where they needed to be spiritually. He gave them the pieces to the big picture about himself from the the Scriptures, but they did not yet see how the pieces fit together. Later they described feeling their *hearts burn within* as he talked with them along the road (verse 32)—the type of excitement that builds when you feel on the verge of discovery, but not quite there yet.

Transition to truth starts when someone comes alongside another sojourner and shares accurately the Word of God. The Scriptures reveal Jesus, the Lord, who is the way, the truth, and the life. He is willing to walk with us when we cannot see him, and invites us to walk with him to see the truth.

Respond
Has someone come alongside and helped you understand truth? Jesus not only spoke truth to these disciples, he brought hope. How has God's Word brought you hope in times of transition?

Prayer for the journey
Lord, thank you for the truth of your Word. Help me to live that truth out in my words and actions today. Amen.

Waypoint 22

A light turns on

So they drew near to the village to which they were going. He acted as if he were going farther, but they urged him strongly, saying, "Stay with us, for it is toward evening and the day is now far spent." So he went in to stay with them. When he was at table with them, he took the bread and blessed and broke it and gave it to them. And their eyes were opened, and they recognized him. And he vanished from their sight. They said to each other, "Did not our hearts burn within us while he talked to us on the road, while he opened to us the Scriptures?" And they rose that same hour and returned to Jerusalem. (Luke 24:28–33a)

A holiday reception at the general's quarters meant a guaranteed delicacy, the legendary-secret-family-recipe: *hammy whammies.* The gracious host and his wife always provided a lavish spread of sweets and treats, but what defined "holiday reception" at their house were the scrumptious, can't eat just one (or two), warm, sweet—with a savory bite!—*hammy whammies.* These receptions make the list of memorable military meals, along with the unit dining-in/mess night, the military ball, and in my husband's case, the MRE with a trooper far from the kitchen table. Food can mark important life moments, as here in Luke 24.

Prior to the meal, Jesus, walking incognito with the two disciples, explained the reason for his sacrificial death from Scripture. To fully transition to truth about Jesus, we start by discovering what the Scriptures say about him. The New Testament reveals the truth about Christ clearly, and Jesus showed these disciples the same truth in the prophecies recorded by Moses and the prophets many years before his birth. He built the foundation for transformation in the hearts of these men.

When the trio reached Emmaus, Jesus acted as if he had further to travel. Moved by their conversation, the disciples pleaded with him to stay for dinner. As they gathered around the table, Jesus, the invited guest, did something out of the ordinary. He assumed the role of the host by taking the bread, blessing it, breaking it, and giving it to them.[37] His action flipped on a light in their minds. Suddenly, they recognized Jesus. From Scripture, Jesus had revealed to them the truth of the plan; now he revealed to them the truth of his resurrected self.[38]

They responded the same way people still respond when we experience that life-changing transition—to know and accept the truth that Jesus is not only a historical figure who changed society, he is also the resurrected redeemer who can transform our life. Even though it was late and they were travel-weary, they journeyed back to Jerusalem to share their experience with Jesus with the other Christ-followers. Their personal encounter with the Lord became something shared by all the disciples.[39]

The meal these two disciples shared with Jesus in Emmaus is one that Christ-followers continue to recount today. The spiritual *whammy* they experienced in that meal is no secret recipe, but it is, without question, legendary and life-changing.

Respond

How did Jesus show his care for the disciples? Read Luke 24 and compare how they felt before and after the meeting. What before and after transitions have you experienced with Jesus?

Prayer for the journey

Lord, help me recognize your voice of truth in my life. Uncover anything that hides your presence from my view. Amen.

Waypoint 23

Saul—Ambushed on the road to Damascus

Read

Now as he went on his way, he approached Damascus, and suddenly a light from heaven shone around him. And falling to the ground he heard a voice saying to him, "Saul, Saul, why are you persecuting me?" And he said, "Who are you, Lord?" And he said, "I am Jesus, whom you are persecuting. But rise and enter the city, and you will be told what you are to do." (Acts 9:3–6)

Reflect

A young military wife deplaned from the transatlantic flight and made her way through customs in Frankfurt Airport with her E4 chaplain-assistant husband and their two young children. Though tired from a restless overnight flight, they were eager to see their new home for the next three years. Her husband was to sign into the replacement center and then they would board the bus for the last leg of their long trip, to the German town of Wurzburg. She spotted him first—a man in uniform holding a sign with her husband's name. As they came closer, she recognized the familiar chaplain's cross insignia, but this was not the chaplain for whom her husband was to be working.

This chaplain had received approval to redirect the E4 and his family—*if* he could reach him at the airport before he signed in. After introducing himself, he announced that the young family would not be going to Wurzburg but to Wiesbaden. Wurzburg was east of Frankfurt. Wiesbaden was west of Frankfurt. Their welcome packet had prepared them for Wurzburg. Their household goods were going to Wurzburg. They knew nothing about Wiesbaden. Their journey to their new home had just taken a 180-degree turn in the opposite direction.

The military can surprise you with abrupt transitions, even in the midst of a change of station. The Lord used a similar tactic to redirect Saul, who would become known by his Greek name, Paul, in the middle of his journey from Jerusalem to Damascus. Saul thought he was doing the right thing in the eyes of God by tracking down and persecuting all the Jews who had become Christ-followers. I would love to have seen the look on his face as that bright light sent him to the ground. He heard the voice of Jesus redirecting his life with a 180-degree turn. In the dust on the road between cities, God began the transition in Saul's life from persecuting anyone following the dead teacher Jesus, to preaching the good news of the risen Savior, Jesus the Lord.

God can begin a spiritual transition in us at a time and in a way that we may least expect. In the middle of a move, after we have pulled up roots, before we have settled, the Lord may ambush you to begin something new or different within you.

By the way, the E4 Specialist and his family left Germany three years later as E6 Staff Sergeant and family. For many years afterward, the couple said that the best thing that happened in their military life was a chaplain ambushing them at Frankfurt airport. No doubt, Saul would say the same of his ambush on the road to Damascus.

Respond
What circumstances or times of military transition such as deployment, PCS, temporary duty, or promotion have facilitated a heart transition in you?

Prayer for the journey
Lord, with each new day give me a heart to know you and serve you more than I did the day before. Change my direction if I go the wrong way. Set my feet on the sure path of your will. Amen.

Waypoint 24

An itinerary change

Saul rose from the ground, and although his eyes were opened, he saw nothing. So they led him by the hand and brought him into Damascus. And for three days he was without sight, and neither ate nor drank. (Acts 9:8–9)

My husband's first deployment to Afghanistan included an unplanned three-day delay in Turkey. His unit took commercial flights to Germany then transferred people and equipment to several different military aircraft to fly to Afghanistan. His aircraft experienced engine trouble and landed in Turkey for repairs. Though he wanted to be with his unit, the three days at the U.S. airbase were an opportunity for my husband to to have his spirit refreshed by fellowship with Air Force chaplains there.

Saul experienced a three-day unplanned itinerary change in his mission's journey. Unlike my husband's refreshing timeout, this was a radical transition. His heart transition was not instant. The bright light he encountered when the Lord ambushed him caused temporary blindness and someone had to lead him by the hand to Damascus. The event affected him so much that he did not eat or drink during this period. As the hours passed, I imagine he wondered how long his blindness would last.

Transition of the heart can be painful, troubling, and can take time. The three days in darkness would have given Saul time to perhaps replay in his mind the encounter with Jesus on the road. He had thought he was honoring God by ridding his religion of any acknowledgement of the radical Jesus, but now he had experienced a divine encounter with this same Jesus. During his sightless days, God was working in him. The Lord gave Saul a vision of a man named Ananias who would come and lay his hands on him to restore his sight.

God could have given Saul this life-transitioning message while he was lying in the dust of the road. He could have immediately restored his sight, but Saul might not have completely processed what had happened if the transition message and restoration of sight had been immediate. He might have continued on his journey shaken, but unchanged.

God knows how to lead each of us through a heart transition, and he knows how long it will take. For Saul it took a blinding ambush while traveling, three days of blindness, a vision while blind, and the touch of another person—Ananias. Saul's transition was so drastic that God used a supernatural occurrence, a physical incapacitation, a spiritual vision, and a human encounter. God orchestrated all these in such a way that Saul would never forget, or doubt, that God was redirecting his life.

Heart transition can be hard work. God knows where he wants us to be in our life journey with him. Sometimes he takes undeniable and unforgettable measures to get our attention and lead us through a meaningful transition.

Respond

Why do you think Saul's conversion experience was so dramatic? What was your life like before you encountered Christ? How have you changed?

Prayer for the journey

(Pray for someone today. Think of someone who, like Saul, is an improbable candidate.) Lord, today I pray for _____, who needs to encounter you. Thank you that they are not beyond your reach. If you could transform someone like Saul, you can transform anyone! Amen.

Waypoint 25

A hesitant participant

Now there was a disciple at Damascus named Ananias. The Lord said to him in a vision, "Ananias." And he said, "Here I am, Lord." And the Lord said to him, "Rise and go to the street called Straight, and at the house of Judas look for a man of Tarsus named Saul, for behold, he is praying, and he has seen in a vision a man named Ananias come in and lay his hands on him so that he might regain his sight." But Ananias answered, "Lord, I have heard from many about this man, how much evil he has done to your saints at Jerusalem. And here he has authority from the chief priests to bind all who call on your name." But the Lord said to him, "Go, for he is a chosen instrument of mine to carry my name before the Gentiles and kings and the children of Israel. For I will show him how much he must suffer for the sake of my name." So Ananias departed and entered the house. And laying his hands on him he said, "Brother Saul, the Lord Jesus who appeared to you on the road by which you came has sent me so that you may regain your sight and be filled with the Holy Spirit." And immediately something like scales fell from his eyes, and he regained his sight. Then he rose and was baptized; and taking food, he was strengthened. (Acts 9:10–19a)

Reflect

When the military sent us to Germany, my language skills were little more than "guten Tag" (Good day). Cautious excitement rose in me when a neighbor offered to tutor me in German if would help her improve her English. The arrangement led to a delightful friendship that also helped me transition my American mind to better understand the language and culture. I might have learned similar lessons from a book, but the human touch was better.

God knows what will move us down life's road to get us in step with his plan. In coordinating Saul's heart transition, God used a person to open his eyes and point him in the right direction. God used supernatural power to ambush and blind Saul, but to complete his heart transition, God sent a person to touch him and speak the words from the Lord. All Ananias did was touch and talk, yet God used him as his agent of change.

Ananias was a hesitant participant at first. How humorous to think that after receiving divine instructions to go and pray for Saul, Ananias informed the Lord about Saul's reputation! Do you think he was asking if Jesus also knew the reports? The Lord did not rebuke him, he just repeated the instructions with clarity.

Heart transition is a God-thing designed for humans. Sometimes we are the ones needing the transition and the Lord uses others to help us. Other times, we are the ones used as part of the transition plan for someone God brings across our path. We may doubt that we can play a significant role in another's heart transition, or we may question a prompting from the Lord to reach out to someone. Sister, don't downplay or overlook the human connection as a part of God's heart transition plan. Whether a simple cultural transition, or a radical spiritual transformation, God can use other people to make it happen. God can use you!

Respond

What role did obedience play in this leg of Saul's spiritual journey? How has God used others in your spiritual journey?

Prayer for the journey

Lord, make me your hand extended to someone today. Speak through me, touch through me, encourage through me. Amen.

Waypoint 26

Daniel—Tips for a successful transition

Then the king commanded Ashpenaz, his chief eunuch, to bring some of the people of Israel, both of the royal family and of the nobility, youths without blemish, of good appearance and skillful in all wisdom, endowed with knowledge, understanding learning, and competent to stand in the king's palace, and to teach them the literature and language of the Chaldeans. The king assigned them a daily portion of the food that the king ate, and of the wine that he drank. They were to be educated for three years, and at the end of that time they were to stand before the king. Among these were Daniel, Hananiah, Mishael, and Azariah of the tribe of Judah. And the chief of the eunuchs gave them names: Daniel he called Belteshazzar, Hananiah he called Shadrach, Mishael he called Meshach, and Azariah he called Abednego. But Daniel resolved that he would not defile himself with the king's food, or with the wine that he drank. Therefore he asked the chief of the eunuchs to allow him not to defile himself. (Daniel 1:3–8)

Reflect

A "greybeard" is not a pirate or Native American chief, but a former military leader sought out by the current leaders for advice. Greybeards cannot make decisions or assume responsibility for the current leaders, but they can share tips and advice from lessons learned when they called the shots.

When it comes to advice on how to thrive in transition, one of the best *greybeards* in Scripture is Daniel. Caught up in a forced transition from freedom in Judah to captivity in Babylon, he became a servant in a foreign king's palace. Daniel's journey yields valuable tips for success in transition by observing what he did, not only to survive, but also to thrive.

Transitions that involve a change in venue will bring new people and new methods. Every new situation is accompanied by adjustment to the "new." Encountering new cultural norms, institutional standards, community traditions, or the personal habits of new neighbors, coworkers, or friends can be disconcerting.

Daniel found himself immersed in a completely new society where the language, people, customs, and religion were all different from his own. Yet, in the midst of all that was new, he determined to maintain the personal values instilled from a child. His new situation required him to study and learn about the local pagan religion. His captors even gave him a different name that referred to a foreign god.[40] Through all of these challenges, Daniel did not waver in what and in whom he believed.

Daniel's choice not to defile himself with the king's food or wine illustrates his determination to stay strong in his values and beliefs. The word *defile* indicates Daniel's choice was an issue of religious faithfulness. His actions were not those of a man out to prove something. Scripture implies (Daniel 1:10–14) that he did not make a public protest or start a culture war by his refusal to eat the king's food.[41] His choice indicated his absolute loyalty to God. His attitude was that of determination and resolution. He learned about the culture, but he did not accept the flattery of the king or dependence on the king, as his acceptance of the king's food would have communicated.[42]

God blessed Daniel through what had to be a challenging transition. Daniel 1:9 reports that God allowed Daniel to gain favor and compassion from those who were responsible for him.

You may not be able to change the standards of a venue to fall in line with God's principles, but you can resolve to hold to those values you believe are pleasing to the Lord.

Sister, may we stand firm in every transition and proclaim, "I know whom I have believed, and I am convinced that he is able to guard until that Day what has been entrusted to me" (2 Timothy 1:12b).

Respond

What situations have challenged your values since you became a military wife? How have times of transition tested the resolve of your values and standards?

Prayer for the journey

Lord, help me stand in godly determination against those things that would harm my relationship with you. Give me wisdom and godly insight as I walk through this day. Amen.

Waypoint 27

Transition is a Team Sport

As for these four youths, God gave them learning and skill in all literature and wisdom, and Daniel had understanding in all visions and dreams. At the end of the time, when the king had commanded that they should be brought in, the chief of the eunuchs brought them in before Nebuchadnezzar. And the king spoke with them, and among all of them none was found like Daniel, Hananiah, Mishael, and Azariah ... (Daniel 1:17–19)

Then Daniel went to his house and made the matter known to Hananiah, Mishael, and Azariah, his companions, and told them to seek mercy from the God of heaven concerning this mystery, so that Daniel and his companions might not be destroyed with the rest of the wise men of Babylon. (Daniel 2:17–18)

Then the king gave Daniel high honors and many great gifts, and made him ruler over the whole province of Babylon and chief prefect over all the wise men of Babylon. Daniel made a request of the king, and he appointed Shadrach, Meshach, and Abednego over the affairs of the province of Babylon ... (Daniel 2:48–49)

Reflect

In the transition from freedom at home in Judah to forced captivity in Babylon, Daniel stood out as a leader among his peers. However, he did not go through this adjustment on his own. His teammates were Shadrach, Meshach, and Abednego.

In the first two chapters of Daniel, we see his team studying together in the School of Babylon. The pagan teachers recognized this Hebrew team for their superior aptitude (1:19). They took a dietary oath together and the team was healthier than any of their peers (1:15). When faced with their first life-and-death challenge in their new positions, they prayed together as a team and God answered their request (2:17–19). When the king rewarded Daniel for revealing the meaning of a dream, Daniel convinced the king to reward the other members of his team as well (2:49). No doubt, Daniel would list good teamwork as a priority for successful transition.

To state that teamwork is important to the military is like saying fuel is important to a car. From a two-person buddy team watching each other's back to the Air Force providing close air support for the Army, the military knows it must function as a team to be successful.

What is in every fiber of military functionality is sometimes strangely missing in the life of some military spouses. Military spouse Shelley Kimball admitted, "As a military spouse, I was making everything so much harder by insisting to myself that I go it alone. I refused help. A lot. Even in desperate times. I thought it was a personal failing, a weakness, to be willing to accept help. I was so wrong. So very wrong."[43]

Transition can go much smoother if you tackle it with a team. Your home team of husband and possibly children will face many major life transitions together. Like Daniel and his team, you can best support each other if everyone signs on to the same shared values to guide your decisions. As Daniel made sure the king not only rewarded him, but also his team, every member of your family needs to know you consider their feelings and aspirations.

In addition to your home team, may I suggest you pull together a prayer team of people not bound by location and distance to back you up? Daniel already had his prayer team in place when a crisis arose. Any time is a good time to build a team to support each other in prayer, but having that team in place before you are in crisis mode is comforting.

Sister, don't go it alone. *Teamwork* can make the *hard work* of transition easier!

Respond

How can you relate to the statement from military spouse Shelley about "going it alone"? How has going through transition with the support and help of others made a difference in your times of transition?

Prayer for the journey

Lord, thank you for those you have sent my way to ease the challenges of transition. Bless them and use us to encourage one another in this journey called life. Amen.

Waypoint 28
The bod pod

Daniel said: "Test your servants for ten days; let us be given vegetables to eat and water to drink. Then let our appearance and the appearance of the youths who eat the king's food be observed by you, and deal with your servants according to what you see." So he listened to them in this matter, and tested them for ten days. At the end of ten days it was seen that they were better in appearance and fatter in flesh than all the youths who ate the king's food. So the steward took away their food and the wine they were to drink, and gave them vegetables. (Daniel 1:12–16)

During a year of advanced military training for which my husband was selected, the health and fitness department offered a deal a spouse could not refuse. In an effort to promote family fitness, the department invited spouses to experience the "Bod Pod." This sophisticated contraption is the gold standard for body composition assessment. I determined this would be my year to get in shape, and the Bod Pod was my first step toward that fitness goal. I threw any claustrophobic tendency out the window as I sat in the futuristic-looking egg-shaped chamber. The Bod Pod would measure my fat and lean muscle mass— what did I have to lose? (no pun intended). The bottom line— again, no pun intended—was that I needed some help when it came to fitness. For weeks afterward when I spotted a fellow spouse with a sad countenance, I only had to ask, "Bod Pod?"

and she would nod forlornly. To their credit, the department worked with us to develop an exercise program and offered suggestions in dietary changes.

Daniel did not change his diet for physical reasons, but for religious convictions. However, the change he made concerning food resulted in prime physical health that was evident to his captors. The step of self-discipline Daniel took was an act of devotion that met with God's approval and blessing.[44] Daniel's choice of food is not included in Scripture for the purpose of following his diet, but for the purpose of seeing God's hand at work in his life. God strengthened him—body, soul, and spirit—to remain faithful even in captivity.

Our bodies matter to God. Caring for them with proper nutrition, exercise, and rest allows us to return our bodies in service to him.[45] Paul exhorts us to "present your bodies as a living sacrifice, holy and acceptable to God, which is your spiritual worship" (Romans 12:1). One way we worship God is to seek to be a good steward of the body he has given.[46]

In times of transition, it takes discipline not to live off fast food. (I'm fond of McD's chicken wrap with a side of fries.) Being good stewards of health is pleasing to the Lord and a positive example to others. Having cut and chiseled abs is not a biblical requirement. Scripture does not equate physical perfection with godliness. However, as in the case of Daniel, good health can be a testimony of your good choices and God's good care.

Respond

How do you integrate exercise into your daily life? What ways have you found to maintain healthy standards of eating and exercise during transitions?

Prayer for the journey

Lord, help me steward the body you have given me. Show me areas to work on so I may serve you in good health. Amen.

Waypoint 29
Open the thanksgiving window

Daniel answered and said:
"Blessed be the name of God forever and ever,
    to whom belong wisdom and might.
He changes times and seasons;
    he removes kings and sets up kings;
he gives wisdom to the wise
    and knowledge to those who have understanding;
he reveals deep and hidden things;
    he knows what is in the darkness
    and the light dwells with him.
To you, O God of my fathers,
    I give thanks and praise,
for you have given me wisdom and might,
    and have now made known to me what we asked of you,
    for you have made known to us the king's matter."
(Daniel 2:20–23)

Reflect

In the midst of the greatest transition ever undertaken by the United States, General George Washington issued a General Order on November 30, 1777 stating in part:

> Forasmuch as it is the indispensable duty of all men, to adore the superintending providence of Almighty God; to acknowledge with gratitude their obligations to him for benefits received, and to implore such further blessings as they stand in need of; and if having pleased him in his abundant mercy, not only to continue to us the innumera-

ble bounties of his common providence, but also, to smile upon us in the prosecution of a just and necessary war, for the defense of our unalienable rights and liberties.

It is therefore recommended by Congress, that Thursday the 18th Day of December next be set apart for Solemn Thanksgiving and Praise; that at that time, and with one voice, the good people may express the grateful feelings of their hearts ...[47]

During a time of war, with all the hardships that it brings, one may wonder why General Washington and Congress would exhort the people of our struggling nation to have grateful feelings in their hearts and express their gratitude to God.

We could pose the same question concerning Daniel, a captive serving in a foreign land separated from family and friends. The United States gave thanks in the middle of the Revolutionary War because they believed God was helping them and would continue to do so. Daniel believed the same. He gave thanks in a time when his life was on the line— interpret the king's dream or die. He gave thanks to God for giving him a revelation of the dream. God's answer to Daniel's prayer showed his personal involvement in Daniel's life. Daniel spontaneously sang a hymn of thanksgiving to God for making wisdom available in his time of need.[48]

In *Girl Meets Change*, former military wife Kristen Strong describes the role of thanksgiving in the midst of transition: "When change wipes all the natural light from the rooms of my heart, being thankful is the way to usher it back in.... We understand that when change plants us in a windowless room, gratitude gives us a window to welcome the light ..."[49]

Praise and thanksgiving is our acknowledgement of God's help and presence. God entered Daniel's situation and brought the light of his power and wisdom. Sister, his wisdom is available to you; his greatness is yours to experience! Hallelujah!

Respond

How can thanksgiving help you thrive in transition? Write your own proclamation of thanksgiving and share it with your family.

Prayer for the journey

"I will give to the Lord the thanks due to his righteousness, and I will sing praise to the name of the Lord, Most High" (Psalm 7:17). Amen.

Waypoint 30
Prayer to the rescue

Read

When Daniel knew that the document had been signed, he went to his house where he had windows in his upper chamber open toward Jerusalem. He got down on his knees three times a day and prayed and gave thanks before his God, as he had done previously. (Daniel 6:10)

Reflect

In the military context, what is the common component of the following: a basic training graduation, an ethnic celebration event, the opening of a new commissary, a change of command, and a retirement ceremony? If you said prayer, you are right. Isn't it noteworthy that at a time when prayer is prohibited in many public places, the military includes prayer in every special event you can imagine? A casual observer might conclude that prayer is a priority in the military. But you cannot deny that prayer was a priority for Daniel.

Most people have heard of Daniel in the lions' den. If you think Daniel prayed a powerful prayer for protection while staring into the snarling teeth of hungry lions, you might be right—but the Scriptures do not mention Daniel praying there. In fact, praying is what got him thrown into the den! Before you decide to avoid prayer as life-threatening, let's look at the story.

Everyone in the kingdom knew that Daniel had a practice of praying three times a day. The officials who were jealous of Daniel tricked the king into signing an irrevocable decree that for thirty days no one could make a petition to any god or man other than the king. Punishment for breaking the decree would mean keeping company with large felines.

Knowing the king had signed the devious decree did not stop Daniel from keeping his appointment with God. He went to his private upper room to pray as he always did. As with his choice of food, he was not making a defiant public spectacle— he was expressing his faith. The phrase *he got down on his knees* lets us know this was a private act, as standing was the common public position of prayer.[50] Daniel's disobedience of the decree was not so much a demonstration of his personal rights as much as a daily practice of personal renewal in the presence of God.

Daniel's advice to us all would be to make prayer a priority. When you settle into a calm routine of life, prayer will refresh your spirit. When you move through the uncertainty of transition, prayer will rescue your soul.

The prophet Jeremiah wrote a letter to the exiles in captivity during the time Daniel lived. Daniel's commitment to prayer followed his admonition.[51] We too can benefit from living by the words of Jeremiah: "For I know the plans I have for you, declares the LORD, plans for welfare and not for evil, to give you a future and a hope. Then you will call upon me and come and pray to me, and I will hear you. You will seek me and find me, when you seek me with all your heart, I will be found by you, declares the LORD ..." (Jeremiah 29:11–14).

Respond
In what way does Daniel's response to the king's decree inspire you? How did prayer help Daniel through transition? How has personal prayer helped you through transition?

Prayer for the journey
Lord, you are near to all who call on you, to all who call on you in truth. You fulfill the desire of those who fear you; you hear our cry and save us. Amen. (See Psalm 145:18–19.)

Notes for Journey 1

1. "Holmes-Rahe Stress Inventory," The American Institute of Stress, http://www.stress.org/holmes-rahe-stress-inventory/ (accessed August 28, 2015).

2. Bill Arnola, NIV Application Commentary: 1 & 2 Samuel (Grand Rapids: Zondervan, 2003), 231.

3. Walter Brueggemann, Interpretation: 1 & 2 Samuel (Louisville, KY: Westminster John Knox Press, 1990), 128.

4. John Woodhouse, 1 Samuel: Looking for a Leader (Wheaton, IL: Crossway Books, 2008), 348.

5. Joyce G. Baldwin, Tyndale Old Testament Commentary: 1&2 Samuel (Downers Grove, IL: InterVarsity Press, 1988), 140.

6. Military.com offers numerous PCS downloadable checklists to help you organize your military move at http://www.military.com/money/pcs-dity-move/pcs-checklists.html (accessed August 8, 2015).

7. Sue Jervis, Relocation, Gender and Emotion: A Psycho-Social Perspective (London: Karnac Books, Ltd., 2011), 53.

8. Ibid, 68.

9. Ralph Klein, Word Biblical Commentary: 1 Samuel (Waco Texas: Word Publishing, 1983), 283.

10. Arnold, 389.

11. John H. Walton, Victor H. Matthews, Mark W. Chavalas, The IVP Bible Background Commentary: Old Testament (Downers Grove, IL: InterVarsity Press, 2000), 518.

12. Craig C. Broyles, New International Biblical Commentary: Psalms (Peabody, MA: Hendrickson Publishers, 1999), 450–451.

13. Broyles, 456

14. Eugene Peterson, A Long Obedience in the Same Direction: Discipleship in an Instant Society (Downers Grove, IL: InterVarsity Press, 2000), 157.

15. Broyles, 470.

16. John Goldingay, Baker Commentary on the Old Testament: Wisdom and Psalms (Grand Rapids: Baker Academic, 2008), 563–564.

17. James D. G. Dunn and John Rogerson, Eerdmans Commentary on the Bible, (Grand Rapids: Wm. B. Eerdmans Publishing, 2003), 42.

18. John Phillips, Exploring Psalms, Volume 2 (Grand Rapids: Kregal Publishing, 2003, 538.

19. Max Anders, Gary Inrig, Holman Old Testament Commentary: 1&2 Kings (Nashville, TN: B&H Publishing Group, 2003), 134.

20. Iain W. Provan, Understanding the Bible Commentary Series: 1 & 2 Kings (Grand Rapids: Baker Books, 2003), 111.

21. Dan McCartney, Baker Exegetical Commentary on the New Testament: James (Grand Rapids: Baker Academic, 2009), 260.

22. Oswald Chambers, *My Utmost for His Highest* (Grand Rapids, MI: Discovery House, 1991), 236,

23. Erin Dooley, "90% of Military Wives Jobless or Underemployed, 'Not Acceptable,'" March 14, 2014, http://abcnews.go.com/Politics/90-military-wives-jobless-underemployed-acceptable/story?id=22720559, (accessed August, 11, 2015).

24. John Vandiver, "Study: 90 percent of military spouses underemployed," Stars and Stripes, February 12, 2014. http://www.stripes.com/news/study-90-percent-of-military-spouses-underemployed-1.267239, (Accessed August, 11, 2015).

25. Michelle Aikman, "Military Life Made Me Question My Identity," http://militaryspouse.com/career/military-life-made-me-question-my-identity, (accessed August 11, 2015).

26. Simon J. DeVries, *Word Biblical Commentary: 1 Kings* (Waco, TX: Word Book, Publishing, 1985), 235.

27. Provan, 144.

28. Ibid., 145.

29. John W. Olley, *The Bible Speaks Today: The Message of Kings* (Downers Grove, IL: InterVarsity Press, 2011), 179.

30. Eric J. Bargerhuff, *The Most Misused Verses in the Bible* (Bloomington, MN: Bethany House Publishers, 2012), 102.

31. F. F. Bruce, *The Book of Acts* (Grand Rapids: Wm. B. Eerdmans, 1988), 249.

32. Gordon D. Fee, *Understanding the Bible Commentary Series: 1 & 2 Timothy* (Grand Rapids: Baker Books, 2011), 2.

33. John Polhill, *The New American Commentary: Acts* (Nashville, TN: B&H Publishing Group, 2001), 298.

34. Clinton Arnold editor, *Zondervan Illustrated Bible Backgrounds commentary: John, Acts* (Grand Rapids, MI: Zondervan, 2002), 130.

35. Susan Miller, *After the Boxes are Unpacked* (Carol Stream, IL: Tyndale House, 2015), 183.

36. Darrell L. Bock, *Baker Exegetical Commentary on the New Testament* (Grand Rapids, MI: Baker Academic, 2007), 272.

37. John F. Walvoord, Roy B. Zuck, editors, *The Bible Knowledge Commentary*, (Dallas: Victor Books, 1983). 398.

38. Philip H. Towner, *The New International Commentary on the New Testament: The Letters to Timothy and Titus* (Grand Rapids: Wm. B. Eerdmans Publishing Co., 2006), 98.

39. Ajith Fernando, *NIV Application Commentary: Acts* (Grand Rapids, MI: Zondervan, 1998), 411.

40. F. F. Bruce, *The Acts of the Apostles: The Greek Text with Introduction and Commentary* (Grand Rapids: Wm. B. Eerdmans Publishing Co., 1990), 536.

Notes for Journey 2

1. Ajith Fernanco, *The NIV Application Commentary: Acts* (Grand Rapids, MI: Zondervan, 1998), 319.
2. John Phillips, *Exploring Acts: An Expository Commentary* (Grand Rapids: Kregel Publications, 2001), 197.
3. William H. Willimon, *Interpretation, A Bible Commentary for Teaching and Preaching: Acts* (Louisville, KY: Westminster John Knox Press, 1988), 96.
4. French Arrington, *The Acts of the Apostles* (Cleveland, TN: Pathway Press, 2004), 178.
5. Arrington, 181.
6. Arrington, 180.
7. Ibid., 178.
8. Willimon, 96.
9. Walter Brueggeman, *The Message of the Psalms* (Minneapolis, MN: Augsburg Publishing House, 1984), 22.
10. John Stott, *The Spirit the Church and the World: The Message of Acts* (Downers Grove, IL: InterVarsity Press, 1990), 189.
11. Arrington, 182.
12. Stott, 189.
13. John E. Hartley, *New International Biblical Commentary: Genesis* (Peabody, MA: Hendrickson Publishers, 2000), 67.
14. Karen H. Jobes, *NIV Application Commentary: Esther* (Grand Rapids, MI: Zondervan, 1999), 55.
15. Margaret Feinberg, *A Time for Everything: Discovering the Beautiful Rhythms of Life* (Nashville, TN: Thomas Nelson, 2013), 7.
16. Karen Jobes, "For Such a Time as This", *Faith & Mission* 14/1 (Fall 1996) 3–13.
17. Ibid.
18. Jobes, 65.
19. Jobes, 102.
20. Frederic Bush, *Word Biblical Commentary, Vol. 9: Ruth-Esther* (Nashville, TN: Thomas Nelson, 1996), 491.
21. Edward F. Campbell, Jr., *Ruth: The Anchor Bible* (New York: Doubleday, 1975), 76.
22. Bush, 95.
23. K. Lawson Younger, Jr., *The NIV Application Commentary: Judges/Ruth* (Grand Rapids: Zondervan, 2002), 422.
24. Ibid.
25. Carolyn Custis James, *The Gospel According to Ruth* (Zondervan, 2008), 34.
26. Bush, 106.
27. Ibid.

28. Bush, 154–155.
29. Taya Kyle, "Note to Self," CBS News, May 22, 2015, www.cbsnews.com/news/note-to-self-taya-kyle-widow-of-navy-seal-chris-kyle/ (accessed August 23, 2015).
30. K. Lawson Younger, Jr., *The NIV Application Commentary: Judges/Ruth* (Grand Rapids: Zondervan, 2002), 490.
31. Bush, 268.
32. Richard Nelson, *The Old Testament Library: Joshua* (Louisville, KY: Westminster John Knox Press, 1997), 180.
33. Marten H. Woudstra, *The New International Commentary on the Old Testament: Joshua* (Grand Rapids: Eerdmans, 1981), 229.
34. Roy Gane, *The NIV Application Commentary: Leviticus/Numbers* (Grand Rapids: Zondervan, 2004), 564.
35. Kenneth O. Gangel, *Holman Old Testament Commentary: Joshua* (Nashville, TN: B&H Publishing Group, 2002), 213.
36. Gane, 564.
37. C. F. Evans, *TPI New Testament Commentaries: Saint Luke* (Philadelphia, PA: Trinity Press International, 1990), 912.
38. Darrell L. Bock, *The IVP New Testament Commentary Series: Luke* (Downers Grove, IL: InterVarsity Press, 1994), 385.
39. Evans, 914.
40. Joyce G. Baldwin, *Daniel: An Introduction and Commentary* (Leicester, England: Inter-Varsity Press, 1978), 80–81.
41. Tremper Longman III, *The NIV Application Commentary: Daniel* (Grand Rapids, MI: Zondervan, 1999), 53.
42. Baldwin 83.
43. Shelley Kimball, "The MilFam Diaries: The Ten Year Lesson," Military Family Advisory Network, June 24, 2014, http://www.militaryfamilyadvisorynetwork.org/the-milfam-diaries/milfam-diaries-ten-year-lesson/ (accessed August 28, 2015).
44. Baldwin, 84.
45. Matthew Lee Anderson, "God Has a Wonderful Plan for Your Body," Christianity Today.com, August 12, 2011, accessed August, 28, 2015, http://www.christianitytoday.com/ct/2011/august/godhasplanforbody.html?start=5.
46. Douglas J. Moo, *The NIV Application Commentary: Romans* (Grand Rapids, MI: Zondervan, 2000), 391.
47. The George Washington Papers at the Library of Congress, 1741–1799, http://memory.loc.gov/cgi-bin/query/r?ammem/mgw:@field (DOCID+@lit(gw100134) (accessed August 31, 2015).
48. Baldwin, 90–91.
49. Kristen Strong, *Girl Meets Change* (Grand Rapids, MI: Baker, 2015), 110–111.
50. Paul M. Lederach, *Believers Church Bible Commentary: Daniel* (Scottdale, PA: Herald Press, 1994), 133.
51. Lederach, 132

Thank you for coming along with Brenda on this encounter with God's Word!

We pray that God will continue to encourage you in the next season of your life. To continue your journey in Scripture, look for the other books in this series:

- **Dedicated: Steps of Faith in God's Plan**

- **Devoted: Steps of Love Toward Healthy Relationships**

- **Deployed: Steps of Hope in Times of Uncertainty**

- **Directed: Steps of Peace in Times of Transition**

You can find them, along with other small group materials and resources to start your own online community at **www.MilitaryWife.bible.**

You can also order free copies of these books for other military wives at **ArmedServicesMinistry.com.**

We need your help...
How has God's Word impacted your life?

Dear Military Wife,

American Bible Society is honored to share this journey with you! Thank you for your selfless devotion to your husband and our country.

Generous contributions from our supporters make it possible for us to provide these resources to you free of charge. As a way of thanking these faithful supporters, we love to share stories of how our Scripture resources have made a difference in someone's life.

 Will you take a moment to tell us about your journey? It's easy online at **ASMFeedback.com**, or, simply scan the QR code for quick access from your device. You can also mail us your response using the enclosed postage-paid card.

You may provide us with your name or remain anonymous.

Thank you and God bless you!

Annie LoCastro
Armed Services Ministry Program Manager
Email: **Provisions@AmericanBible.org**

Check out our website for other devotions:
www.MilitaryWife.bible